"If our contemporary (and it's making the natu it to a psychologist to g(dinning is the psychologist and in this wonderfully moving and intelligent book, she provides exactly the right analysis. And more: she also provides a therapy, in fact a cure, if this civilization could only have the courage to listen to her. Now we may perhaps begin."

—KIRKPATRICK SALE, author of
The Conquest of Paradise: Christopher Columbus and the Columbian Legacy

"Chellis Glendinning urges us to remember who we are as humans and to praise Creation."

—MAUREEN MURDOCK,
author of *The Heroine's Journey*

"In the face of global human and ecological crises, Glendinning makes an important contribution to the much needed conversation about redefining 'progress.' I resonated with her call to re-establish harmony with the rhythms and freedoms of the natural world."

—LINDA JEAN SHEPERD, author of
Lifting the Veil: The Feminine Face of Science

"My Name Is Chellis & I'm in Recovery from Western Civilization."

Chellis Glendinning

SHAMBHALA
Boston & London
1994

to Marc,
deer Marc Kasky

Shambhala Publications, Inc.
Horticultural Hall
300 Massachusetts Avenue
Boston, Massachusetts 02115

9 8 7 6 5 4 3 2 1

First Edition

Printed in the United States of America on acid-free paper ∞

Distributed in the United States by Random House, Inc., and
in Canada by Random House of Canada Ltd

Glendinning, Chellis.
My name is Chellis, and I'm in recovery from western civilization /
Chellis Glendinning.—1st ed.
p.   cm.
Includes bibliographical references and index.
ISBN 0-87773-996-X (alk. paper)
1. Nature—Psychological aspects.   2. Human ecology—Psychological
aspects.   3. Civilization, Modern—20th century—Psychological
aspects.   I. Title.
BF353.5.N37G54   1994   93-39136
155.9'1—dc20   CIP

Earth: isn't this what you want,
an invisible re-arising within us?

—Rainier Maria Rilke, *Duino Elegies*

Contents

Preface: My Name Is Chellis

M Y name is Chellis. I'm in recovery from western civilization.

This is funny, right? I repeat it every time I speak at a recovery conference, psychological seminar, or political gathering about what is fast becoming the screaming link between pervasive personal dysfunction and the ecological crisis. A good laugh always arises from the crowd, something like a hiccup in a Buddhist *sesshin*. The truth about that hiccup is that just about everybody I know who is serious about personal healing, social change, and ecological rebalancing is in recovery: recovery from personal addiction, childhood abuse, childhood deprivation, the nuclear family, sexism, racism, urban alienation, trickle-down economics, combat service in the trenches of the gender wars, the threat of extinction, linear thinking, the mind/body split, technological progress, and the mechanistic worldview.

In the face of this overwhelming onslaught, an equally overwhelming question arises: what on Earth is wrong with us?

You and I are not people who live in communion with the Earth, and yet we are people who evolved over the course of millions of years—through savannah, jungle, and woodland—to live in communion with it. We exist instead dislocated from our roots by the psychological, philosophical, and technological constructions of our civilization, and this alienation leads to our suffering: massive suffering for each and every one of us, and mass suffering throughout our society.

As individuals, we express this suffering in our personal lives, in our relationships with ourselves and each other, by the numbing and abuse of dysfunctional behaviors. Drinking ourselves to oblivion. Shooting up drugs. Raping our babies. Gunning down strangers. Mental-health professionals tell us that a whopping 96 percent of our families suffer from dysfunction of one sort or another, and that the disorder is imprinted and carried on from generation to generation.

As a society, we express our suffering in our relationship with the Earth by the numbing and abuse we enact through ecological destruction. Mowing down forests. Blanketing valleys and mountains with deadly poisons. Spewing garbage into rivers. Building machines to exterminate life. Scientists today tell us we may have only ten or twenty years left to turn around the practices our civilization is employing to destroy the Earth.

It is well past time for us to come home, to return to the matrix from which we came, to recover what we have lost, to remember again the wisdom and balance of the natural world.

My Name Is Chellis & I'm in Recovery from Western Civilization represents my best thinking and feeling about this homecoming. This is a book about getting back to our roots: about why such a return is crucial for our survival, how we can begin this journey, and what personal and ecological rewards will come to us when we do. This is a book that highlights two of the most important social issues of our times: the psychological/spiritual challenge each of us is facing, and the ecological crisis besieging our planet. My purpose in revealing the interconnections between these two realms is to encourage a conscious coalescing of the social forces that are addressing them: today's psychological movements (which include the addiction/recovery field, humanistic/transpersonal psychologies, and the burgeoning interest in spirituality in all its earthly forms) and the environmental movement (with its varied devotion to protest, clean-up, conservation, and sustainability).

I write this book as a mental-health professional who has researched personal issues of healing and recovery, as well as global issues concerning the psychological impacts of environmental disaster. But I am not just a detached observer. I also write this book as a fellow traveler through this endangered world we share. As a psychologist I am hardly surprised that through the years the content of my professional interest in social issues has mirrored the unraveling of my awareness of my own personal history. My first embarcation into the world of writing, *Waking Up in the Nuclear Age*, warned of the psychological repercussions of living with the impending disaster of the arms race.[1] "Wake up!" I pleaded, and while I was writing this book, I was attempting to wake myself up in my first exploration of long-term psychotherapy.

My second book, *When Technology Wounds*, concerned the psychological healing pioneered by people exposed to life-threatening technologies like nuclear radiation, chemical pesticides, and toxic waste.[2] As I was writing this book, I was healing my own body and psyche from trauma caused by the technological assaults of oral contraceptives and the Dalkon Shield intrauterine device—and also by assaults I did not yet understand, but that I later learned were metaphorically parallel to the abuse of technology.

In *My Name Is Chellis & I'm in Recovery from Western Civilization* I excavate deeper. I pierce beyond symptoms like nuclear warheads and Dalkon Shields to the core psychosocial dynamics underlying the creation of such abusive technologies and the myriad other abuses that characterize our society. As mirroring would have it, just as I embark upon this work, the core dynamics underlying my most momentous trauma stream into consciousness: I am flooded with long-repressed memories of my father, a doctor, subjecting my brother and me to brutal torture, "medical" experiments, and sexual assault.

The personal is political. We learned this in the women's movement in the 1960s and '70s. The planetary is personal, the personal planetary. In a kind of interplay of mutual causation, the themes we play out in our private lives mirror those we are exposed to in our society, and vice versa. Could there be a relationship between nuclear war and wife battering? Between alcoholism and toxic contamination? Between global warming and workaholism?

As eco-philosopher David Abram writes, "With thousands of acres of nonregenerating forest disappearing every hour and hundreds of species becoming extinct each month as a result of our excesses, we can hardly be surprised by the amount of epidemic illnesses in our culture, from increasingly severe immune dysfunctions and cancers, to widespread psychological distress, depressions, and ever more frequent suicides, to the growing number of murders."[3] Highlighting the other side of the dynamic, environmental educators William Devall and George Sessions reveal what lies, too often unspoken, at the edge of our consciousness: "The environmental problems of technocratic-industrial societies are beginning to be seen as . . . a crisis of character and culture."[4]

From both ends of this dynamic, our dysfunctional practices are calling out to us to awaken to the parallels between the numbing and abuse we express in our individual lives and that of our collective relationship to the life of our planet. But let us be alert as we explore such a perception: in the midst of this mass technological society we inhabit, making declarations about returning to the Earth to address our human pathologies can never succeed so long as they remain mere pleas to step outside and smell the grass. Our declarations must constitute radical acts with far-flung implications for the ways we live and how we perceive ourselves as living beings. I am reminded of Lewis Mumford's assertion in his "Prologue to Our Time," written originally in 1962 and published in *The New Yorker* in 1975: "Progress indeed!"[5] Mumford spent a lifetime analyzing and critiquing the fundamental metaphor shaping western technological civilization—The Machine—and indeed he meant to suggest an overhaul of the entire system. As one of his ardent students, I pick up on this worthy pursuit and press it even further than my mentor did.

In the first section of this book, "Roots," I explore the immutability of our human relationship to the natural world and track the psychological and social benefits of this relationship.

In "Domestication and Its Discontents," I investigate the origins of our severance from the natural world, and I use the psychological construct of post-traumatic stress to illuminate its effects upon our psyches, culture, and society. Because of the built-in displacement of our lives from the Earth, I maintain that a traumatized state is not merely the domain of the Vietnam veteran or the survivor of childhood abuse; it is the underlying condition of the domesticated psyche.

In "Hunting, Gathering, and Healing," I apply principles of psychological recovery toward a vision of collective recovery.

Last, in "Re-Arising within Us," I posit that full recovery reaches beyond the realms of both psychological healing and social change; it involves a return to the reciprocity, power, and wildness of our earthy nature which, despite all, still resides in the cells of our bodies—and, despite all, is still champing for expression. The time is long since past for us to remember and call upon the passion for life we are capable of knowing when we live, not bolstered in the solid steel encasement of a world made of machines but breathing fully in intimacy and rhythm with the Earth.

Ahéheé

IN the Diné (Navajo) language, the word Ahéheé carries a sense of appreciation similar to that expressed by the English phrase "Thank you." Ahéheé , though, is used not simply as an interpersonal exchange; it is used as an expression of gratitude in the context of the spirit of all life.

Sitting at my big writing table in Tesuque, New Mexico, I came into an understanding of such an inclusive sense of appreciation: I could not have opened to these experiences, thought these thoughts, or written this book without the backing and parallel work of my beloved community. I owe an intellectual debt to many of these people: as always, the late Lewis Mumford; Jerry Mander, Jeannette Armstrong, Simon Ortiz, Frances Harwood, Theodore Roszak, Reina Attias, Kirkpatrick Sale, John Mohawk, Susan Griffin, and Larry Emerson. Paul Shepard deserves special attention. I thought I'd never encounter another thinker to rival Mumford in depth of passion and sweep of vision, and I have.

The land of northern New Mexico has taught me as much as any conversation or book. All hail to Tesuque and Ranchito de Melodia! And to my nature teachers: the jackrabbits, piñon trees, October moonrises, Dimid Hayes, Thor Sigstedt, Roosevelt, and Bear.

Gratitude goes to my special friends and colleagues for their encouragement and their work: Marc Kasky, Suzan Harjo, Adele Getty, Francis Huxley, David Abram, Carole Roberts, Craig

Comstock, Johanna Maybury, Claire Greensfelder, Bill Keepin, Annie Prutzman, Jo Eberl, Elinor Gollay, Tyrone Cashman, Yana Ross, Dominique Mazeaud, Robert Matthews, Clark Kimball, Gary Dewalt, Victor di Suvero, Colin Franklin, Missy Martin, Carl Anthony, and Deena Metzger. Frances Harwood brought her anthropological expertise to the subjects of agriculture, the neolithic, and cultural relativity. Margaret Ehrenberg was kind enough to make suggestions for research on the development of pastoral societies, and Greg Pleshaw helped with permissions.

Alvino Waconda, Manuel Pino, Anna Rondon, and Claire Kowemy have given me more inspiration than they can understand. Phil Harrison and Ervin Nakai expanded my world with their caring, dedication, and love of adventure.

I have to invent a special category of thanks for Steven Schmidt, whose enthusiasm for the project and advice about the publishing world went far beyond the call of friendship. I extend my appreciation to Kay Carlson for her agility at the keyboard, and to the folks at the Cafe Romana for their little island of Italian zest.

I am grateful to those whose support has been financial: the Foundation for Deep Ecology, Gene Knudson-Hoffman, W. H. Ferry and Carol Bernstein Ferry, Marc Kasky, the Fort Mason Foundation, and Alice Hasler.

Claire Greensfelder, Gene Knudsen-Hoffman, Tracy Puett, Tyrone Cashman, Kirkpatrick Sale, Laura Sewall, Jeannette Armstrong, Gary DeWalt, and Frances Harwood read all or parts of the manuscript and gave invaluable feedback.

I am indebted to Shambhala Publications: to Jonathan Green for his recognition of the book's potential; to Emily Sell for asking the right questions and editing with down-to-earth insight; to my old Cafe Mediterraneum pal Brian Boland for his artistic genius; to David O'Neal for overseeing the editing process; to Carl Walesa for copy editing; to Sam Bercholz for history and for the future. Thanks too to John Raatz of the Visioneering

Group for his unbounded enthusiasm for public relations and to Lindsay Holt III for his brilliance and photography.

Finally, I can never express enough gratitude to the dedicated healers whose intelligence and faith have brought me through: Robin Murphy, Reina Attias, Don Smith, Pam Suhre, Jim Klemmer; most especially, my brother, Sandy Glendinning.

The entire manuscript was written on the reverse sides of my last book's galleys with a Blackfeet Indian Earth Pencil.

PART ONE

Roots

The way we stand, you can see we have grown up this way together, out of the same soil, with the same rains, leaning in the same way toward the sun. See how we lean together in the same direction. How the dead limbs of one of us rests in the branches of another. How those branches have grown around the limbs. How the two are inseparable. How if you look you can see the different ways we have taken this place into us. Magnolia, loblolly bay, sweet gum, Southern bayberry, Pacific bayberry, wherever we grow there are many of us, Monterey pine, sugar pine, white-bark pine, four-leaf pine, single-leaf pine, bristle-cone pine, foxtail pine, Torrey pine, Western red pine, Jeffrey pine, bishop pine.

> —SUSAN GRIFFIN,
> *Woman and Nature*

The arch of the sky
And mightiness of storms
Encompasses me,
And I am carried away
Trembling with joy.

> —Inuit (Eskimo) song

1

People and Nature

In short, all good things are wild and free.

—HENRY DAVID THOREAU

WHEN I was twelve years old, I had an experience for which my life in TV-drenched suburbia did not prepare me. I had a vision. While ambling through a Cleveland city park on my way to softball practice, my sight suddenly clarified and I could see that all the discarded artifacts of civilization, in fact the very gum wrappers and cigarette butts surrounding me at that moment, were overwhelming the natural landscape. I stopped, momentarily transfixed in the awe of reflection, and the words of a poem came to me:

Everywhere she looks she sees man.
Beer bottles broken under trees,
Smokestacks against dirty skies,
Cars and highways, trains and bomber planes.
Man makes rivers turn black,
Man makes war.
Has man gone too far?
Everywhere she looks she sees man.

The year was 1959.

In 1954, nine-year-old David Haenke had an equally unexpected moment. Haenke, who is now a full-time environmental activist, tells it this way: "I was very young, and there was no obvious precedent," he says. "No one was telling me about ecology or Gaia. There was no Earth Day and certainly no talk about nature and mystical experience. Yet it happened. . . . It was the fall in Freeland, Michigan. I went for a walk with three other boys, and I sort of trailed behind. Suddenly, unexpectedly, I began to feel as if I were no longer in ordinary reality, but in a great cathedral. Red and yellow leaves on the trees, the crunch of leaves under my feet, the warm air, the smell of grass: time became enchanted. I walked slower and slower so I could feel this kinesthetic immersion. I was in a state of wonder. We walked for an hour, and for an hour I was in an enchanted universe."[1]

In 1988, at age forty-five, educator Carole Roberts also experienced something that surprised her. She had been hired to coordinate an expedition to film a reforestation project in Costa Rica. As she tells it, "There's this ever-present sense of change going on in the jungle. The humidity is 100 percent, everything is rotting, and there are lots of things that can hurt you: some of the most dangerous vipers in the world, bugs that deposit worms in your body. You can't just sit down on the ground, you have to look around and see what's there. . . . After a few weeks I noticed that something was happening to me. I was feeling more at home in this place *because* of the way it required me to be alert and present. One morning, sitting on the porch and listening to the chattering of birds and animals, I found myself speaking with a parrot in calls back and forth. It was so natural, at first I didn't even know I was doing it. It was as if I was becoming dispersed into the environment, like a hallucinogenic drug experience in which there is a reduction of ego so you can feel a direct experience of other. . . . When I returned to my urban existence in San Francisco, I was rushing across a college quadrangle in a hurry to some meeting or other. Suddenly I noticed that everything here was laid out—manicured lawn, little hedges on one side, flowers in boxes—and *I burst into tears!* I had this sudden, overwhelming flash of loss and longing. Here the presence of life was reduced and controlled in a way that felt unacceptable. I felt, and I still feel, deprived."[2]

Healthy, Wholly

What's happening here? How do people with no previous environmental knowledge come to feel at home in the natural world and even, in its presence, break through to unintended nonordinary states of awareness? In a society that delivers a near-airtight prescription for rational living and technological progress, how is it that we come to sense that something is wrong or missing?

People have a natural state of being. It is variously known as "being integrated," "human potential," and "merging mind, body, and spirit." Taoist philosophy refers to this state as the "balance of yin and yang." To Lakota (Sioux) Indians, it is known as "walking in a sacred manner;" to the Diné (Navajo), "standing in the center of the world." I call this state of being our *primal matrix*: the state of a healthy, wholly functioning psyche in full-bodied participation with a healthy, wholly functioning Earth. This is the *anima mundi* which resides both within us and all around us. In a society fraught with psychological distress, in which certain forms of dysfunction like workaholism and sexual addiction are accepted as normal and nearly everyone manifests some truncation of full maturity, using a special word to describe the seemingly rare and elusive healthy psyche becomes more than helpful; it becomes necessary.

And what is this healthy state? From the perspective of the individual, it is a bodily experience, a perception of the world, and an attitude about being alive that is characterized by openness, attunement, wonder, and willingness in the here and now to say YES to life. It is a sense of ease with who we are and fulfillment with what we do, and when it is alive and thriving, it is how we feel most hours of most days in most circumstances. Our primal matrix is the part of us that says YES to the future. It welcomes the stages of the life cycle that present themselves as we grow from infancy through adulthood to old age, moving through each developmental phase so that we mature into the dynamic human beings we were meant to be. Our primal matrix contains within its sphere the ability to heal ourselves. When we encounter strain and hardship beyond the expected conflicts and trials of being alive, we are able to muster extraordinary resources to pass through these times with resilience, perhaps even clarity, or, after the fact, to recover from their lingering ill effects.

We who exist in the midst of the dysfunction and uncertainty of the technological world find ourselves wondering about such a way of being—perhaps in silent moments, perhaps in unrelated fragments. As our lives are upset by more personal crises and the Earth is marred by more ecological disasters, we find our quiet wonderings growing, taking on greater urgency, becoming loud and pressing questions. Why don't we feel good? Why is there so much fear? Why are life-affirming experiences and resources so elusive for us? The answer to such questions is perplexingly simple: we have access to the love for life, equanimity, and resilience that are inherent in the primal matrix when our lives are embedded—with all of Creation's animals and greens, insects and microbes, rocks and roots—in the rhythms of the Earth. We are fully who we are when we live in the natural world.

Caught in the clutches of a society that is characterized by dislocation and abuse, our primal matrix becomes nearly lost to us. Perhaps we are reminded of its existence when we have the opportunity to witness, or meet, tribal peoples who are open, vibrant, and fully participating in life, or when we encounter our own elders who have made their way into old age with dignity. Most importantly, we remember it for ourselves when its power peaks through to our awareness, when we sense the magical aliveness of tender buds bursting on spring trees, when we feel a bond while gazing into the eyes of a furry animal, when we approach the tasks before us with a mindfulness that reverberates throughout our bodies.

Our primal matrix is also reflected back to us in our ability to say NO. It is what makes us know in our gut, without ever being told about justice or right and wrong, the difference between caring and abuse. Anthropology writer Jean Liedloff tells a marvelous story about this capacity for discrimination.[3] In the Yequana tribe in Venezuelan Amazonia, she writes, the children are trusted, from the moment they begin to crawl, to take care of themselves. They are free to roam about the jungle independently, to climb and play by rushing streams, to go wherever they wish to go, to test themselves against total independence. Despite this long-standing freedom, one day a tribe member named Tududu decided to build a playpen for his two-year-old son. According to Liedloff, the invention was made of sticks and vines; from her civilized perspective it looked like "a comic strip version of a prehistoric playpen." When it was finished, Tududu lifted his son into the contraption, and in an instant the boy was screaming horrific sounds rarely heard in this forest. As Liedloff puts it, "It was unequivocal. The playpen was *wrong*." Tududu immediately pulled the child out and smashed his invention to bits. The primal matrix had spoken loud and clear: NO! The boy had rejected forced confinement, and Tududu had received the message.

This same innate understanding of what is wrong is what causes us all to know, however consciously or unconsciously, that a childhood spent in the emotional chaos of an alcoholic family is a travesty, that pumping toxic materials like dioxin and mercury into a river is violence, that our world is in deep trouble. It is what so many of us are seeking, perhaps without ever articulating it, when we strive to save endangered animals or "work" personal recovery programs. It is a deeply rooted knowledge of our inherent limitations and our grandest potentials, of what hurts and what is healthy. It is an inner knowing about who we are.

In today's world the existence of such a primal presence may seem a distant and long-lost memory. Our knowledge of its wisdom becomes muddied by the daily onslaught of appointments and traffic jams, by a socialization process that unabashedly trains us to mistrust our own feelings and perceptions, and most pointedly, by the layer upon layer of psychological entanglement, bereavement, and disorientation in our own hearts. Meanwhile, in the latest and perhaps most subtle effort at suppression of the primal matrix, university-taught deconstructive and New Age "you-create-your-own-reality" ideologies are training people to deny the existence of human universalities and a preference for well-being in favor of superficiality, absolute relativity, and meaninglessness. To those of us who recognize, or even vaguely suspect, that life is made of more than another appointment, another technical gadget, another theory, or another "experience," questions arise—questions that do indeed strive to identify universalities, champion a preference for health, and find meaning in life.

Did we, with these bodies and these psyches, evolve to exist in a setting distinct from the mass technological society so many of us assume as reality?

Were we built to experience a different kind of world than we now know?

What are we so urgently pursuing when we try to heal the wounds that plague our psyches?

What are we battling for when we fight to clean up toxic pollution?

What is natural to us?

To approach questions like these solely in the context of our civilized mind-set automatically truncates our ability to find answers. We are instead called upon to enter into territory that resides outside currently accepted conceptions of reality and is, therefore, strictly taboo. Yet this territory may offer the clearest access we have to the last remaining vestiges of our primal matrix. This is the domain—the psychological knowledge, the social practices, the spiritual understandings, the ecological awareness—of nature-based peoples.

Let me clarify. When I use the word *nature-based*, I mean people who live, or have lived, in direct, unmediated participation with the forces and cycles of the natural world. I mean indigenous people who practice today, or practiced in the past, a combination of foraging plant foods, scattering seeds, hunting, fishing, and scavenging. I mean people who perceive this Earth to be a sacred place and live accordingly. I mean, in the parlance of anthropology, hunter-gatherers.

Not surprisingly, most of us remain naive about such people; we are *supposed* to be naive about them. Our culture gives us few opportunities to know them as they know themselves, while it exposes us to legions of stereotypical, incorrect, and derogatory concepts and images. We *are* aware that they, as well as all other indigenous peoples, are being exterminated at a phenomenal pace. In 1492, an estimated fifteen million native people, many of them hunter-gatherers, inhabited the territory that is now the United States. Through slaughter, slavery, relocation, disease, and the demise of the buffalo, the total had diminished to 237,000 by 1900;[4] today it is 1.9 million.[5] In Africa the hunter-gatherer !Kung are being overrun by technological encroachment, private property, corporate development, and government projects. Deforestation in Borneo is destroying the habitat of the nomadic Penan. Ninety of Brazil's original 270 tribes have disappeared in the wake of economic development and the demise of the rainforest, while more than two-thirds of the remaining groups have populations of less than one thousand people each. A Massachusetts Institute of Technology study by linguist Ken Hale estimates that of the world's six thousand native languages, only three hundred have a secure future.[6] Julian Lang, a Karuk from northern California, reports that in 1992 only three people still spoke the Karuk language.[7]

Against this backdrop, it is not easy to gather knowledge about nature-based people, or any native people for that matter. I garner as much as I can from archaeological and anthropological records about groups of the past. I gather information from ethnographic research on contemporary nature-based peoples— although still-intact communities are increasingly rare and a truism among anthropologists asserts that we take giant leaps of faith when we extrapolate from today's nature-based cultures to those of twelve thousand or three hundred thousand years ago. I also gather information from stories, insights, and reports given to me by Native American friends and colleagues in touch with their cultures.

Throughout this effort, a definitive focus guides my delving: I am riveted on the lessons of the hunter-gatherer experience. Yet I listen carefully to *all* native peoples because, whether they are farmers, pastoralists, or land-based peasants, they share a far closer link than we to a way of living that at one time was the *only* way people survived on this planet.

The taboo against looking seriously at native cultures is crack- ing open. Since the quincentennial anniversary of Christopher Columbus's arrival in North America and the United Nations Decade of the World's Indigenous People, native peoples all over the planet have seized this uncommon opportunity to educate the rest of us about their crises of survival and *the validity of their ways of living.* If one quality defines technological ideology, though, it is the narrowness of its conception of reality. Despite this growing tendency to ask fundamental questions about hu- man nature, most people, and certainly most institutions, still use technological progress as *the* standard for human values and ways, unmindfully calling all other societies—from hunter-gatherer to agricultural and early industrial—"primitive," "undeveloped," or "developing."

The Blackfoot architect Douglas Cardinal turns this insistence on linear superiority on its head, writing: "It is imperative that people understand the separate reality of Native peoples and the rest of society."[8] In resonance with this perception, I draw a distinction that places nature-based cultures in one category of the human experience—and all other arrangements, from early agricultural to technological, in another. I know. Such a perspective is upsetting to the accepted view of human evolution as an exclusively progressive process. It is equally upsetting to the conviction that technological society belongs in its own distinct category while all other cultures exist merely in transition toward it. The reason for such an unconventional approach is this: in the west, the changes that took place in our psyches and our relationship to the Earth when we abandoned our long-standing practice of nomadic foraging in favor of the sedentary life of controlled planting and animal husbandry were completely unprecedented. Because of the psychological, social, technological, and ecological changes this unprecedented way of life initiated, a ball was set rolling that in time gathered force and speed, ultimately becoming the mass technological civilization we inhabit today. Despite their differences, at the level of psychological functioning and ecological awareness nature-based cultures have more in common with each other than with all other social arrangements.

I will explore these changes and commonalities in later chapters, but for now suffice it to say that the act of honoring nature-based cultures for what they have to model and teach about human potential does indeed pose a radical challenge to today's accepted way of living, thinking, perceiving, and experiencing. In a desperate and long-enduring effort to extinguish any hint of this challenge, modern peoples and institutions have disavowed, warned against, blunted, and crushed knowledge of native ways (whether of wise women in sixteenth-century Europe or of Tsa-la-gi [Cherokee] peoples of nineteenth-century America). They have created a virtual maze of negative falsehoods about them and relegated any remaining curiosity to dimly lit museums and children's books.

"Hunter-gatherers are always hungry," we are told. "People who lived in the woods were lucky to live past age twenty," we repeat. "Why should we care? There aren't any Indians left," we dutifully tell each other. "But the human mind *must* push the envelope and invent new technologies! It's our nature!" Such socialization is so deeply rooted that even those who ask the kinds of questions that crack through the rigid mind-set of technological society sometimes fall prey to its power. After seeing the film *Black Robe*, social philosopher and author Jerry Mander told me about his disappointment at the depiction of Native Americans in the film. "Those are Haudenosaunee [Iroquois] people," he said. "The bloody savagery highlighted between the two tribes is how the white conquerors wanted, and still want, the Indians to be seen. But the movie didn't even hint at the cooperation that existed between the tribes, or the democratic modes of government they had developed among themselves. And it didn't explain the terrible conflict colonization caused among them."9

In a flash of embarrassment I realized that because I had been relentlessly accused of naïveté for championing nature-based peoples, when I saw *Black Robe* I had bent over backward to embrace what everyone else seemed convinced is the "universal" and "continuous" brutality of "human nature" which, in a civilization as universally and continuously brutal as ours, is considered a given. But isn't this just the point? As a society we don't *know* what the Haudenosaunee reality was or is, and what it meant and means to the Haudenosaunee people. We aren't challenging the stories we've been told or the movies we've seen. We aren't even allowing ourselves to reside in uncertainty about possible answers; we are clutching the old stereotypes.

Yet, at the same time, our collective psychological state and the ecological state of our Earth are presenting us with glaring symptoms of the devastated condition of a once-thriving primal matrix, urgently demanding that we ask questions not only about the way we perceive people who live in organic relationship with the Earth—but about who we humans are.

Our Human Past

Life on Earth began some 3.5 billion years ago as chains of DNA, RNA, and protein assembled themselves into minute threads and spheres of blue-green algae and bacteria. Primitive mammals evolved as recently as 190 million years ago, and it is estimated that anthropoids, from whom we humans directly evolved, came into existence some 60 million years ago. And humans? The earliest stages of our emergence seem to have taken place in what is now East Africa, where the first recognizably humanlike beings emerged from our anthropoid ancestors 8 million years ago. The first skeletal evidence we have of these creatures is 4 million years old, and the first preserved artifacts are 2.5 million years old. The first humans who resemble us exactly in body shape and hair distribution came into being some forty thousand years back.

When we attempt to construct a time line of the history of this evolution, we run head-on into a controversy among physical anthropologists and paleontologists about the length of time of human existence—some saying we have been human for 3 million years, others for a more conservative forty thousand years. Despite the heat rising from this dispute, I am going to risk laying out a time line and picking a point when our humanness came into being. I am going to say that humans have been human, living in close approximation to our current state of biological and psychological development, for 1 million years.

Visualize a distance of one hundred feet: the length of a basketball court plus six feet more. Imagine that this distance represents the last 1 million years of existence of the creatures who have become *Homo sapiens*. Fasten your seat belts: the last *one-fifth of an inch* of this hundred feet represents the length of time that we have lived in mass technological civilization, with the assumptions about life and reality that you and I are taught to assume as "normal." Not very long, and conceivably not very normal.

Another way to think about this time span is by generations. Over the course of 1 million years the human lineage has passed through some thirty-five thousand generations. It may surprise you to realize that the Industrial Revolution began just *six generations* ago. For people engaged in recovery from addiction or trauma, one of the first things we learn is to reclaim our family lineage by tracing dysfunctional behaviors back through the generations. A recovering drug addict might discover that his father was a raging alcoholic who had been beaten by his father, who was traumatized in combat in World War I—and so on back as long as family memory and documentation provide information. Alex Haley's television miniseries *Queen* reveals the proximity of the social and economic problems, psychic effects, and coping strategies of today's African-Americans, and the violence, lynching, and psychic abuse African people endured during slavery and abolition.

For me, this process of generational reclamation showed that the technological world we assume as so absolute is a mere wink in the grand expanse of human history. In my mid-forties, I have had face-to-face relations with four of the six generations that have lived since the beginning of the Industrial Revolution: that of my Edwardian grandparents, who were born in Ohio in the 1880s; that of my parents, who came of age during the depression; mine, the postwar baby boom of the 1940s; and that of our children, who were born in the 1970s and '80s. And I've heard stories about the fifth generation, my grandparents' parents who predate the Civil War.

Another notable point on our time line is the period when humans stopped living wholly in the wilderness and first started to manage and control nature's "products" and "resources" by constructing artificial barriers between human life and the natural world. Domestication. In the Near East, in the uplands surrounding the rivers Tigris and Euphrates, and in southeastern Europe, organized planting and animal husbandry laid the foundation for what later became western Euro-American civilization some ten thousand years ago. On a one-hundred-foot time line this is just *one foot* from present time; in terms of human lineage, it is a mere *three hundred generations* ago.

One of the facts we tend to forget from our situs within a civilization that insists on instant satisfaction is that evolution is a long, rambling process. No one fully understands how it works, yet it is clear to physical anthropologists and paleontologists alike that human beings evolved over thousands upon thousands of generations in complex chemical, molecular, and energetic synchronicity with the other animals, wind currents and solar patterns, rainfall and lightning. It was a full 60 million years, and 2 million generations, between the development of our direct anthropoid precursors and our emergence as thinking bipedal creatures. During this stretch of time, just as our bodies evolved to sport opposable thumbs, grow hair over certain parts and not over others, and have face-to-face sexual contact, so our psyches developed to think, feel, intuit, and sense, to energetically mirror the passage of the moon, and to seek guidance and resolution by dreaming of Earth, sky, and animal.

Evolutionary changes do not take place or reach completion in six generations, or in three hundred. Living within the confines of the western world, we have unabashedly taken the concept of evolution, which describes a lumbering process involving fur, bodily fluids, DNA, electromagnetics, and a complex interlinking of the evolution of many species, and in a desperate rush to project instant gratification, we have translated it to mean that people can mutate to unprecedented heights of mechanization in a single quantum leap. Look at the messages heralded by the culture around us. We are constantly being told, and many of us believe, that we are superior to the natural world (and certainly to people who wear animal hides) and that our supercomputers, space shuttles, biotechnologies, and virtual realities will facilitate the final escape from our earthly origins. Yet as we gaze at the full expanse of our history, as we see the one-fifth inch of technological civilization and one foot of domesticated effort against the backdrop of what basketball star Michael Jordan would tell you is a *long* distance, we stand in one of those stark confrontations with truth that many of us would rather avoid: *our primal matrix grew from the Earth, is inherently part of the Earth, and is built to thrive in intimacy with the Earth.*

2

Primal Matrix

i am the throat
of the sandia mountains
a night wind woman
who burns
with every breath
she takes

—Joy Harjo, "Fire"

WHAT happens to our experience of life when we live in intimacy with the Earth? Might we know bodily felt contentment most of our days? Might we know when to say yes and when to say no, what to pursue and what to let pass by? Might the kinds of perceptions that broke through to David Haenke, Carole Roberts, and me be common everyday happenings?

Before we venture into the forbidden territory of our taboo to see what we can learn about these questions, let me be up-front. Idealization of nature-based people looms as a constant temptation, a kind of knee-jerk flip side to the denigration so potently drummed into us. I definitely mean to bolt open our eyes about the psychology, social practices, and ecological awareness of nature-based people. I do not mean to forget that life is difficult, snow is unbearably cold, people everywhere are given to imbalance and conflict, and animals can devour human flesh. Now, to our taboo.

As far as we can tell from anthropological documentation and anecdotal stories, nature-based people are psychologically open. They have to be. Their survival in the wilderness depends on a sharp attunement to the world around them: to the scent of pollen riding the wind, the drift of ice down a cold creek, the angle of sun streaming through the trees. For the most part, the berries, greens, nuts, roots, and animals nature-based people seek are concealed from sight; to find them they must attend to the world with ears, eyes, noses, and skin alive and alert.

Pre-1940s anthropologists placed people who live in direct participation with the natural world on the lowest rung of an evolutionary ladder they invented, dismissing them outright with words like *childlike*, *savage*, and *primitive*. Despite a more enlightened view held by today's anthropologists, such a perspective lingers in the popular imagination. Once we challenge this perception, though, we see that it is a clever way of deflecting some rather obvious observations. For instance, as a group authentic nature-based people are not neurotic, repressed, or burdened by psychopathology as we know it; rather, they tend to be integrated in thought, feeling, and spirit. They live in the moment, unafraid to laugh uproariously and grieve wholeheartedly. They are intelligent, remembering vast amounts of information about the relationship between animals' habits, plants' life cycles, the passage of stars, and their communal histories, and are able to integrate this data into complex, constantly developing cosmologies. From the earliest age, each child learns to remember complicated instructions, long stories, and patterns of inquiry that prepare him for survival in the wilds. Bruno Maser, the Swiss rainforest activist, reports that when the Penan people of Borneo depart from camp, they erect a wooden stele for the next arriving tribe, carving into it elaborate instructions about available foodstuffs, water, weather, and when the area was last inhabited.[1]

(I stretch my imagination by guessing what it might be like if everything I have committed to memory—the street layouts of major American cities, for instance; the changes in body style of European, Japanese, and American automobiles; an embarrassingly high percentage of questions on the TV game show *Jeopardy*; my social-security number, telephone credit-card number, quick-cash bank number; Southwest Airlines's flight schedule between Albuquerque and San Francisco—if *all of it* were replaced by knowledge of the seasons and creatures of the natural world.)

Most pointedly, nature-based people manifest the very qualities that contemporary psychotherapy, the recovery movement, and spiritual practices continually aim for: a visible sense of inner peace, unselfconscious humility, an urge to communal cooperation, and heartfelt appreciation for the world around them. Having studied Solomon Islanders, lived with the Balinese, and trekked through Nepal, anthropologist Frances Harwood describes this way of being as "a transparency of psyche, a wide-openness that emanates a space and time far beyond what we associate with the individual."[2]

Jean Liedloff tells of a journey through South American jungle that illuminates this transparent quality. This was a journey undertaken by five Yequana Indians, two Italians, and Liedloff herself in a huge dugout canoe. For her Italian colleagues, the trip was marred from the moment of inception by the looming prospect of a half-mile, boulder-laden portage that, they knew from past experience, would be grueling.

Liedloff describes the portage:

Here before me were several men engaged in a single task. Two, the Italians, were tense, frowning, losing their tempers at everything, and cursing nonstop in the distinctive manner of the Tuscan. The rest, Indians, were having a fine time. They were laughing at the unwieldiness of the canoe, making a game of the battle, relaxed between pushes, laughing at their own scrapes and especially amused when the canoe, as it wobbled forward, pinned one, then another, underneath it. The fellow held bare-backed against the scorching granite, when he could breathe again, invariably laughed the loudest, enjoying his relief.

All were doing the same work, all were experiencing strain and pain. There was no difference in our situations except that we had been conditioned by our culture to believe that such a combination of circumstances constituted an unquestionable low on the scale of well-being, and were quite unaware that we had any option in the matter.

The Indians, on the other hand, equally unconscious of making a choice, were in a particularly merry state of mind, reveling in the camaraderie; and of course they had no long build-up of dread to mar the preceding days.[3]

To understand what appears to be a consistent contrast between westerners' and nature-based peoples' baseline psychological capabilities, we will do well to explore three dimensions of consciousness that are inherent to the primal matrix. I like to think of these levels of awareness in terms of specific psychic qualities each of us can identify from our own experience. Interestingly, the psychiatrist Stanislav Grof has created a map that reveals three realms of psychic experience that closely correspond to these same qualities.

The first quality is *a sense of belonging and security in the world, trust, faith.* We might call this the consciousness of I-in-We, for it encompasses a sense of self in the context of relationship. Correspondingly, Grof speaks of the perinatal matrix,[4] the archetypal challenge to individuation we each face during the process of being born: the passage from in utero oneness, through the terrifying life-or-death struggle that takes place in the birth canal, to the liberation of arrival. If all goes well, the lesson of this initiation is the discovery that a sense of belonging and connectedness can be reinstated afterward.

A second quality of the primal matrix is *a sense of personal integrity, centeredness, capability*: the consciousness of I. To Grof, this is the biographical, the terrain of personal development.[5] When the inborn needs we each harbor for personal development are met, we grow to function well, meet the demands of daily life, participate gracefully in community, and find ourselves capable of mastering the successive challenges of development.

A final psychic quality is *the capacity to draw vision and meaning from nonordinary states of consciousness*. Grof calls this terrain the transpersonal.[6] "We Are All One." Self as world, world as self. This realm concerns the We: the vast and essentially mysterious universe we are a part of—all its creatures and beings; past, present, and future; time and space; the life energy.

It makes sense for us to describe these three qualities as separate realms of consciousness. When we experience them, though, each has the capability of transmuting itself into a fourth state of consciousness, an elliptical sense of connectedness that is made up of all three qualities seemingly poured like liquid into a pool of perception and experience much larger and more fluid than each alone.

Nature-based people claim all three of these psychic dimensions, and their sum total, as natural attributes that are theirs by dint of the fact that they live wholly in the natural world. We, on the other hand, ever plugged into our electronic terminals, concrete freeways, and statistical abstractions, huff and puff to reclaim these same capabilities in our weekend workshops, psychotherapy sessions, recovery meetings, and spiritual practices—and then lose them again the moment we turn on the nightly news. What is this essential difference between nature-based people and ourselves? Human well-being and wholeness depend on, and exist in constant and complex intimacy with, the well-being and wholeness of the Earth. So long as we are set apart from participation in that intimacy, we are severed from fully knowing trust and security, authentic self-esteem and skillful means, the larger meanings of life—as well as the overall sense of connectedness to which these qualities transport us.

The Beautiful Trail

The original psychic realm of the primal matrix is *the ability to feel connected and secure*. As Grof points out, we first experience this quality in the womb and then must struggle to refind it after the birthing process. In his work on the stages of psychosocial development, psychoanalytic theorist Erik Erikson explains that we are challenged again in infancy to strengthen the presence of security and trust.[7] As babies, either we are welcomed into a world of caring and belonging or we are not, and barring major psychotherapeutic effort or spiritual breakthrough in later life, our lifelong notion of security is formed based on which of these alternatives occur.

Nature-based cultures welcome infants into the world in a way, writes Liedloff, "appropriate to the ancient continuum of our species, inasmuch as it is suited to the tendencies and expectations with which we have evolved."[8] To begin, the inherent fact of human insecurity is implicit in the thought of nature-based people. "Original human beings are the ones who are dream and Earth—and are torn from the land," explains Okanagan educator Jeannette Armstrong. "This is part of our philosophy. *We are torn from the land*."[9] Implicit too is a comprehensive approach to restoring the security the birthing process interrupts.

The nature-based woman gives birth naturally, without the invasion of chemical drugs, fluorescent lights, or mechanical forceps. Because she is usually nourished by an organic diet and in fine athletic shape, her labor may be less strenuous than it is for us, and therefore less stressful for the infant. Plus, birthing often takes place in a ceremonial setting, with drums, chanting, and medicinal herbs to support mother and child through the process.

Next, the fullness of security that has been temporarily lost by the relative violence of birthing is conscientiously reinstated. Whether by mother, aunt, older brother, grandmother, or father, infants are carried everywhere no matter what task the adults are engaged in: foraging, tending the fire, paddling a canoe, preparing food, or dancing in ceremony. Babies are included in community activities and constantly exposed to the changing sounds, textures, and temperatures of the world: human voices, birds singing, wind rustling through the branches. As psychohistorian Paul Shepard writes in his ground-breaking book, *Nature and Madness*, "The unfiltered, unpolluted air, the flicker of wild birds, real sunshine and rain, mud to be tasted and tree bark to grasp, the sounds of wind and water—all these are not vague and pleasant amenities for the infant, but the stuff out of which its second grounding, even while in its mother's arms, has begun."[10] Consistent with the mysterious way of synchronistic interplay and mutual causation in the natural world, this feast of interwoven motion, sound, and texture provides a rich stimulus for each child's psychoneurological development.

The nature-based mother also nurses her baby on demand any time of night or day until the child reaches age three or four. Here is the news that is old hat to nature-based people, and yet is so astounding to us as to be almost unbelievable: *each child is held close to someone's body almost every moment of life from birth until she indicates she is ready to crawl*. Nature-based children come to know life as an experience of security and connectedness in a way we can barely imagine.

At the same time, each child is also welcomed into a conceptual world that gives meaning to these experiences. As psychohistorian Morris Berman observes, "The view of nature was that of an enchanted world. Rocks, trees, rivers, and clouds were all seen as wondrous, alive, and human beings felt at home in this

environment. The cosmos, in short, was a place of belonging."[11]
Repeated songs, prayers, stories, and chants teach and reinforce
this understanding of life, as in this well-loved Diné prayer:

> *Now Talking God*
> *With your feet I walk*
> *I walk with your limbs*
> *I carry forth your body*
> *For me your mind thinks*
> *Your voice speaks for me*
> *Beauty is before me*
> *And beauty is behind me*
> *Above and below me hovers the beautiful*
> *I am surrounded by it*
> *I am immersed in it*
> *In my youth I am aware of it*
> *And in old age I shall walk quietly*
> *The beautiful trail.*[14]

To nature-based people it is the Earth, and the community of
living beings it sustains, that provide the ultimate source of
security. The Earth generates all sustenance; it is the beginning
and end of all life, the great round of which we are a part. To
native people the words *environment* and *nature* reflect an absurd
and false separation. Seneca educator John Mohawk tells a story
that, even in its revelation of imminent danger, speaks of this
interweaving of wild and human.[12] One night Mohawk was
awakened in his home in upstate New York by a phone call. It
was 3:00 AM. On the other end of the line a group of Australian
aborigines, agitated and afraid, begged for his help. A mining
corporation had arrived in their ancestral territory with plans
to drill into the sacred mountain, they explained. But to them,
this mountain was a great sleeping lizard whose job was to
dream their existence. The problem: the drilling would *wake the
lizard up.* . . .

As Paula Gunn Allen of Kwa' waik (Laguna Pueblo) writes, "Beauty is wholeness. Health is wholeness. Goodness is wholeness."[13] Historian Calvin Martin highlights this elliptical way of perception in his book *In the Spirit of the Earth*, pointing out the presence of safety in a world not perfectly safe in the overarching wholeness of the life force and the give-and-take among its parts:

> The human equivalent of the wolf-caribou, wolf-moose, wolf-place relationship is the hunter's conviction that all *out there* is self. To kill for survival becomes a transformation rather than a murder. Certifying it as a transformation is the fact that it is eaten—very important. In this manner, moose becomes me, and I become moose, and so forth with every edible creature I snare or trap or spear or net or gather from this teeming landscape where my imagination and powers are embedded. This, I feel, is the best way to view the metaphysics of the hunting-and-gathering proposition. The meal is sacred; it is mythic (the First Meal, while reminding me of my everlasting kinship with these beings); it is the bringing forth of new life, that of the communicant becoming now, in the process, part of the creature (plant or animal) consumed. . . . It is rather like the transformation that occurs during the masked dance: the adorned dancer has actually become the creature that is being depicted in mime and likeness; the dancer is transformed, translated, because this is the law of the earth.[15]

The welcome each child born into nature-based culture receives is powerful indeed. The inborn expectation of symbiotic contact is so satisfied, the sense of belonging so deeply felt, that each child becomes self-reliant far more rapidly than we imagine possible. Liedloff tells of small Yequana children, and even crawling babies, who are given complete freedom to supervise themselves to play near cliffs, sinkholes, and rushing rivers—and they do not fall in.[16] Hopitu (Hopi) children learn that the fire is hot not by restrictions enforced by adults, but by exploring for themselves.[17] Children in the forest Hill Pandaram tribe are so self-reliant that by age five or six they are ready to leave their parents' care to take on communal responsibilities.[18] Because the early developmental urge for connectedness is so thoroughly answered, there remains no further need to strive to attain it; it is known and integrated. The young people who emerge from such an infancy demonstrate a built-in sense of security—and no need to construct a seat-of-the-pants ego to accomplish the next challenges of life.

Stalking the Wild Asparagus

The development of personal integrity and centeredness is the second ingredient of the primal matrix to concern us in our search to understand psychological health. Developmental theorists identify this quality as an all-important component of the process of individual maturation. The words they use to describe it tend to be confused, though, owing largely to a bias within our society that springs from the high value we place on individualism and ego development.

According to modern psychology, the goal of development, or for that matter of psychotherapy, is to construct a solid sense of boundary. A boundary is a rigid demarcation: a fence, a national border, a property line, a suit of armor or a Giorgio Armani suit, a well-fed ego, a psychological defense mechanism. Just as our political and economic system views the Earth as territory to be acquired, parceled, used, and defended, so our conception of psychological boundary casts the primal matrix as terrain to be demarcated, enclosed, armored, and then, for all the alienation that results, bolstered. Within this unprecedented context the natural urge of the child to explore and develop qualities such as initiative, competency, and identity becomes not the development of centeredness it has been for generations and generations; it becomes the property of the individual, who either successfully encases, or fails to encase, these traits within his personality.

The insights arising out of today's codependence theory provide some of the clearest understanding of the lack of personal integrity of the contemporary psyche. Originally codependents were seen as the "enablers" in relationship with alcoholics; their "support" provided support for the continuation of the disease rather than for recovery. Today the mental-health field sees codependence as part of the overall addictive pattern of modern life, appallingly pervasive in parent-child and work relationships, friendships, and marriages. According to psychotherapist Anne Wilson Schaef, "since codependents feel they have no intrinsic meaning of their own, almost all of their meaning comes from outside." They "literally do not know *where they end and others begin*," and so they "frequently use relationship in the same way drunks use alcohol."[19] One commonly heard joke depicts the codependent lover, after sex, asking her partner, "Was that as good for me as it was for you?" In some codependence recovery programs, participants are so unaware of themselves that in order to function, they have to memorize and commit to following a list of rules for behaving noncodependently: for instance, "speak only for yourself"; "let other people make their own decisions"; "explain what you need."

The emphasis in codependence therapy is rightly placed on today's epidemic of confusion concerning intrapersonal and interpersonal relationships, but the problem is treated by encouraging the development of boundaries that encase the individual and thus defend him from connectedness. Rather than projecting hard demarcations and enclosures onto the natural world, nature-based people define social space by centers that they move through, depart from, revolve around, and return to—sacred sites, water holes, pathways, mountains, caves, gathering places. The nature-based psyche is likewise organized around a sense of centeredness, with the quality and size of each person's field of existence expanding, intensifying, waning, retracting, and over-lapping according to situation and need. Each person is a center of the life force, a star, a microcosm of the whole; each person maintains integrity while flowing transparently through the stream of life.

From this perspective, relating to others presents an entirely different prospect. The task is not defined by boundary, knowing "where I end and the other begins." It is defined by center, knowing *where I begin*. The essential ingredient is not a fence or a wall; it is a constellation of energy emanating from one's being, infusing one's consciousness, ever changing and fluid. When we feel such a space in ourselves, or we feel ourselves to be such a space, our existence takes on the clarity of morning sky after all-night rain. No rules delineating appropriate behavior are required; we *know* who we are, what we feel, how to behave in respectful relationship.

Liedloff tells a story about such clarity that would strike awe in the heart of anyone struggling with the urge to codependence. She was faced with the task of performing minor surgery on a young Yequana tribesman who had developed gangrene. "The pain must have been excruciating," she reports. "While offering no resistance to my scraping the wound with a hunting knife, he wept without any sign of restraint on his wife's lap. She . . . was completely relaxed, not putting herself in her husband's place at all, but serenely accessible, as he buried his face in her body when the pain was greatest or rolled his face from side to side on her lap as he sobbed. The eventual presence of about half the village at the scene did not appear to affect his reaction either toward self-control or dramatization."[20]

This same sense of personal centeredness is integrated, and encouraged, within most nature-based cultures. In Tanzania individuals of the Hazda tribe go off alone for weeks at a time to roam, gather, and hunt.[21] On a group expedition when a Ye-quana boy suddenly and unexpectedly decides to stay in unfamiliar jungle by himself, the others continue on without question.[22] Among the Hill Pandaram, according to anthropologist Brian Morris, "individual men and women are often self-sufficient," and even the elderly take care of themselves,[23] while in Africa the Nyae Nyae !Kung approach their neighbors' marital disputes by attempting to alter the context surrounding conflict so that the combatants themselves are the ones, by their own volition, to change the dynamic.[24]

Knowing such a center is not meant to be a rare or spectacular event. It is an ongoing, natural, Earth-given aspect of our primal matrix. Its development in each of us is instinctive when we grow up in a culture that honors and encourages human participation in the natural world. The satisfaction of our inborn need for security and belonging lays the ground for the development of an authentic sense of personal centeredness. The urge to develop individual capabilities is then given full reign via unfettered freedom to explore. The process of developing one's center is assisted as well by initiation rites. These are experiences structured to help young people cross from childhood into adulthood, often by presenting them with rigorous and dramatic challenges for testing their initiative, competency, will, and balance.

Finally, the development of one's integrity comes about by the stark fact of existing not in the human-built, technology-defined environs of a city that we constantly, if unconsciously, identify with our humanness—but in the wilds which we perceive as foreign and decidedly *not* human. How, other than knowing where I begin, can I find and successfully traverse the next dry rock in a rushing stream? Stalk a wild asparagus? Receive a message about winter's arrival from a flock of birds cawing in the August sky?

As Shepard puts it, "The wilderness environment is mostly given. For the hunter-forager, this Me in a non-Me world is the most penetrating and powerful realization in life. The mature person in such a culture is not concerned with blunting that dreadful reality but with establishing lines of connectedness or relationship. . . . The separation makes impossible a fuzzy confusion: there is no vague 'identity with nature,' but rather a lifelong task of formulating—and internalizing—treaties of affiliation."[25]

A relationship with ourselves and the world based on integrity through energetic affiliation rather than the erection of boundaries presents a fundamental challenge to western psychology. One realm ripe for rethinking is our conception of the encapsulated, individualized self, but the truth of the matter is that we do not have the words to intelligently discuss the issues that arise. To nature-based people, what we call the psyche or individual consciousness does not even exist. Rather the essential unit of wholeness, if we can even use such language, is the entire universe; vital consciousness resides both within us and at the same time all around us in the world. Carl Jung and James Hillman have both nudged western psychology toward acknowledgment of this understanding with their emphasis upon the soul of the world, and according to the wisdom of cultures one million years in the making, we are all a part and expression of the primal matrix of this Earth. At the same time, each of us must discover the uniqueness, capability, and responsibility that allow us to survive—either as functioning members of the human community or, if necessary, alone in the wilds. For nature-based people the healthiest relationship to the natural world, and to each other, is not one of projection or idealized "melting into" with no distinction or definition. It is one of communion: mature interdependent association that honors both individuality, separate needs, and unique modes of expression *and* the seemingly paradoxical fact that we are essentially, whether black-tailed jackrabbit or crystal rock, whether Yami or Eastern European, made of the same stuff.

Cracking to Sacred Reality

When our desires for belonging and integrity are given supportive conditions for development, the basics of personal and communal health are laid down: our day-to-day consciousness functions at its best; we are able to live meaningful lives together; and we have a solid base from which to approach the remaining challenges of personal and social development. But there is more to consider in our quest for well-being, a third dimension of the primal matrix. This is the realm Stanislav Grof calls *nonordinary states of consciousness*. These are states of mind we cannot necessarily explain by the presence of personal security or integrity—in fact, they are often alarmingly active for people who have neither—but they are states that require both of these qualities for successful integration.

The function of nonordinary states of consciousness seems to be the catalyzing of spiritual awakening, psychological breakthrough, and physical healing residing in the realm of archetypal experience and cosmic reality. These are ruptures of one's ordinary perceptions that can result in rearrangements of one's energy field so that healing or revelation takes place. From his experience as a psychiatric researcher, Grof makes a comprehensive listing of such states, naming experiences such as vivid memories of one's long-dead ancestors, trance states revealing guidance for healing, unexplainable synchronistic events, miraculous feats of athletic prowess, and full-bodied identification with universal archetypes.[26]

With its demand for quantifiable evidence and laboratory-verifiable proof, the western scientific bias tends to refute the validity of such events. Yet, despite denial and rejection, they have occurred since time immemorial and continue to occur—often spontaneously, as they did for David Haenke, Carole

Roberts, and me. As Paula Gunn Allen puts it, "The westerner's bias against the nonordinary states of consciousness is as unthinking as the Indian's belief *in* them is said to be."[27]

Nonordinary states of awareness are commonplace, meaningful, and fully integrated into nature-based consensual reality. They are seen as perfectly natural, emerging not just for medicine men and the specially chosen but for everyone, not just at singular moments but regularly. The fact of living in the natural world has much to do with the prevalence of such occurrences. Many of us experience a change in awareness when we are in the wilds, even for short periods of time. We become slower, calmer, more attuned. Our sense of time may decelerate to the point where we detect a spiritual presence in juniper trees or notice the rhythm of intimacy between the yucca blossom and the bee. Our dreams may become more vivid. We may find ourselves talking to birds. I like to let my imagination explore what living *an entire lifetime* in the natural world might be like, since hiking just three miles through the foothills of the Sangre de Cristo mountains produces a radical alteration in awareness, while the psychic changes that take place during a week in the wilderness cannot even be approached with the words available to me in the English language.

In recent years mental-health professionals specializing in trauma and addiction recovery have discovered the healing power of conducting treatment programs in the wilderness. It is here that the continuum of nature's rhythms and textures inspires a renewed sense of receptivity, while direct communication with nonhuman beings expands awareness. The civilized psyche, unnourished by the sense of belonging and clarity of definition natural to the nature-based person, survives by bolstering and armoring the ego and therefore is often incapable of what Carole Roberts refers to as "direct experience of other." Spending time in the wilds offers the opportunity to soften this construction and reconnect with a primordial fluidity not just in ourselves, but in

relation to the creative flux of all things. Even when this recon-
nection is experienced during a brief weekend retreat, the result
may be the closest many of us come to knowing the depth of
fulfillment we are capable of. The ingredients of this fulfillment
are the sense of belonging, energetic self-definition, and ability to
tap into nonordinary realities we have been discussing: the capability to know and express the I-in-We, the I, and the We of the
primal matrix.

Nature-based cultures catalyze, focus, and harness such an
awareness by creating a coherent science and technology dedicated to the daily practice of spiritual knowledge, healing, and
ecological living. Educator Greg Cajete, a Tewa from Khaa po
(Santa Clara Pueblo), challenges the notion of the supremacy of
western empiricism by redefining science as "the process by
which *any* culture makes nature and life accessible to reasoned
understanding."[28] Allen validates this approach. "[The native
attitude] is based very solidly on experience," she writes, "and it
is experience which is shared . . . by most of the members of the
tribal group. It is experience which is verified by hundreds and
thousands of years of experience, and it is a result of actual
perception—sight, taste, hearing, smell—as well as more indi-
rect social and natural phenomena."[29]

As Cajete describes it, the kind of science developed by indigenous people starts from the premise that the Earth is living and
all facets of life upon it are sacred. It sees "all aspects of humanity
in continuous and dynamic interrelationship with every other
aspect of self and environment."[30] Such a science includes research technologies—what we might call catalysts to nonordinary states of awareness such as fasting, herbs and psychotropic
plants, sweat lodges, ceremonies, and quests into the wilderness.
Medicine people and healers are trained to specialize in the
knowledge of this science, and it also includes systems of thought
that are available to everyone. These define the human place in
the universe as one of respectful belonging and provide a basis for

unmediated communication with the forces of the natural world via extraordinary states of consciousness.

This concept of "unmediated communication" with natural beings is difficult for us to grasp. Our notion of psychological possibility is limited by both a rigid definition of self and belief in a system of abstract symbols said to hold predictable meanings for that self. Yet when nature-based people speak of dreams, visions, spirit visitations, bodily knowings, ceremonial unity, and guidance received from animals and plants, they are not speaking of imaginary or halluncinatory experience, projection, or the stuff of the collective unconscious. They are speaking of actual events, of reality, of a world that is as viable and verifiable as the soil beneath their feet. They are speaking of knowing these events, this reality, this world; and they are speaking of using the guidance they receive from it for living sanely and sustainably on this Earth.

According to Allen, "the four mountains in the Mountain Chant do not *stand* for four other mountains. They *are* those exact mountains perceived psychically, as it were, or mystically. Red, used by the Oglala, doesn't *stand* for sacred or earth, but *is* the quality of being, the color of it, when perceived 'in a sacred manner' or from the point of view of earth itself."[31]

At his hand-built house on Diné Nation land, educator Larry Emerson tells me a story about his work as a healer-diagnostician that has implications both for the multitude of levels of consciousness we are capable of and for the integration of these states into everyday living.[32] When, in walking the land, Emerson locates a medicinal herb that has revealed itself in ceremony for use in a specific healing, he does not immediately snatch the plant out of the soil. His awareness shifts once again, his breath quieting, his eyes brimming with tears, to determine the grandmother tree or being of this place. He then asks blessing from this being to take the herb, and only then harvests it for human use.

Holding up a turquoise necklace to the sunlight, Emerson also explains that, to those who have eyes to see, these beads reveal the entire cosmology of his tribe. When worn, this bright necklace descends from the wearer's neck down his chest to a gathering point below the heart; from that point two shorter strands hang down another two or three inches. This necklace speaks of his people's sense of sacredness, he says, its honoring of both humanity's responsibility and its humility in the face of that power. The two sides of the necklace are the complementary dualities of female and male, visible and invisible, Earth and sky, inner and outer, human and nonhuman.

Emerson then brings my attention to a crucial point. When he travels from Diné country to Ute territory, he says, he stops to honor the transition from one terrain to the other. The difference between the tribes that inhabit these territories is not the shape of their necklaces; the archetypal nature of the reality each people lives by is essentially the same. What marks the difference between Diné and Ute is the fact that the land each inhabits is distinct. The birds, rocks, and trees of each land have spoken to each people through what we would call nonordinary states of consciousness. The birds, rocks, and trees have advised them how to create cultures that express the universalities of human life, while respecting each community's unique location on the Earth and therefore each community's unique expression of the life force.

Likewise, the mind of nature-based people—with its sense of belonging and trust, its essence of centeredness, and its ability to crack open to sacred revelation—is a creation woven in continuous communion with both the natural world and the kind of human community that grows out of that communion. This is our primal matrix. It expresses everything we need to know about who we are. It tells us where we belong, why we struggle to heal ourselves, and why we care about the Earth.

3

A Lesson in Earth Civics

My father carves, dancers usually. . . . He holds the Buffalo
Dancer in the piece of cottonwood poised on the edge of his
knee, and he traces—almost caresses—the motion of the
Dancer's crook of the right elbow, the way it is held just below
the midchest, and flicks a cut with a razor-edged carving
knife. . . . He clears his throat a bit and sings, and the song
comes from that motion of his carving, his sitting, the sinews in
his hands and face and the song itself. . . .

Stah wah miayanih, Muukei-lra Shahyaika,
duuwahsteh duumahsthee Dyahnie guuhyouiseh urah-ah.
Wayyuuhuunah wahyuuhuu huu nai ah.

. . . When my father has said a word—in speech or in a song—
I ask him, "What does that word break down to? I mean,
breaking it down to the syllables of sound or phrases of sound,
what do each of these parts mean?" And he has looked at me
with an exasperated—slightly pained—expression on his face,
wondering what I mean. And he tells me, *"It doesn't break down
into anything."*

—SIMON ORTIZ, "Song/Poetry
and Language"

yey? at stim? put (all things in the world are right)

—Okanagan phrase

CULTURES, past and present, that maintain beliefs and practices based on a respectful relationship with the natural world share more than a set of common cosmological qualities; they share a set of common social practices. These practices are of special interest to us because they model the very social forms we long for, struggle to reproduce—yet rarely seem to attain. What occurs when human beings live in intimacy with the Earth? The kind of society we formulate is likely to be participatory, democratic, equalitarian, leisurely, ecological, and sustainable. Like the elliptical wholeness of the natural world, such social practices shape and are shaped by the psychic state of the people, springing from healthy psyches and simultaneously guarding against the emergence of psychological aberrations like addiction and abuse.

Making Glass on the Solomon Islands

Full participation in the life and survival of the group is one of these social practices. In nature-based cultures, nearly everyone is an expert, or at least competent, in nearly every activity the people engage in. By contrast, few of us are competent, much less expert, at more than a few minor activities that contribute to the functioning of our society. To make things worse, as our technologies become more complex and our society increasingly fragmented, we become less competent. An astoundingly small percentage of us knows how to record a television program on a VCR, repair an electronic device, or decipher a Publishers Clearinghouse prize notification. "This is the plan for a B-1 bomber," Candice Bergen states on the 1993 Sprint television ad. "This is the plan for DNA, and this is a long-distance calling plan. What do they have in common? You can't understand any one of them!" Meanwhile, the only activities we seem to share are shopping, driving, and watching television. Such a predicament is not how humans evolved.

According to anthropologist Stanley Diamond, the average man of the hunter-gatherer-pastoral African Nama people is "an expert hunter, a keen observer of nature, a craftsman who can make a kit bag of tools and weapons, a herder who knows the habits and needs of cattle, a direct participant in a variety of tribal rituals and ceremonies, and he is likely to be well-versed in the legends, tales, and proverbs of his people." Diamond goes on to say, "The average primitive . . . is more accomplished, in the literal sense of that term, than are most civilized individuals. He participates more fully and directly in the cultural possibilities open to him, not as a consumer and not vicariously but as an actively engaged, complete person."[1]

Frances Harwood learned about such participation during her field work in the Solomon Islands in the early 1960s.[2] One day, she relates, an assemblage of villagers paid a visit to her hut. They sat down on grass mats on the floor and said to her, "Ever since you came here, you have been asking us a lot of questions. Now we would like to ask you a question." Harwood perked up in attention. "Please . . ." pleaded one tribesman as he picked up the glass she had brought with her. "How do you make this?" "Oh yes, well . . ." she sputtered, trying to bring together the right native words to communicate the process. "It's quite simple. You take sand and you heat it up with fire, and then you mold the glass." "Ah-*ha*!" the islanders responded, enthusiastically nodding their heads and passing the glass around the circle. "Then we'll meet you down at the beach tomorrow at dawn—and you'll show us how to make a glass."

Harwood was stunned. Already struggling to communicate in a language she had barely mastered, she now flailed as she attempted to describe such labyrinthian phenomena as industrial process, factory manufacturing, and division of labor. Her guests grasped none of what she said. They did, however, grasp her refusal to meet them on the beach. Thereafter, they let it be known among the villagers that Harwood's real purpose in coming to the islands had been revealed: she had been sent because she was an incompetent, incapable of doing the simplest things in her own culture.

Turning through the Air

Democracy is a second practice shared by nature-based cultures. In a democratic system every single member of the group has the opportunity to participate in decision-making. You and I clearly value and long for this opportunity. The cries for democracy that rang across the world in 1989 from Eastern Europe, the Soviet Union, and China, and the psychic reverberations these cries caused among millions of others, have constituted one of the most passionate statements of the twentieth century. Yet truly satisfying participatory democracy seems always to evade our reach, even for those of us who inhabit one or another of the great "democracies" that emerged with the Enlightenment.

The crux of the matter is a little-appreciated factor: *scale*. Democracy is automatically abrogated when any gathering of people becomes too numerous for the continuous involvement of each member. As Austrian political philosopher Leopold Kohr puts it, "When something is wrong, something is too big."[3] In a more humorous comment about the unwieldy hierarchies and bureaucracies that accrue in even the most well-intentioned democractic nations, social critic Kirkpatrick Sale writes, "If a mouse were to be as big as an elephant, it would have to *become* an elephant—that is, it would have to develop those features, such as heavy stubby legs, that would allow it to support its extraordinary weight."[4]

Small, face-to-face groups are a universal characteristic of nature-based cultures; in fact, this quality is what defines them. According to anthropologist Joseph Birdsell, five hundred people is the model size of nature-based groups in aboriginal Australia, with fifteen to fifty inhabiting each local band within that larger grouping.[5] At the time of Columbus's arrival in North America, it is estimated that fifty-six people inhabited every fifty square miles along the California coast. In the Southwest the number of people for every fifty square miles was fourteen, while east of the Mississippi it was nine.[6] The average number of people per square mile among all documented hunter-gatherer groups is one.[7]

Democratic decision-making is likewise a common characteristic among nature-based peoples. Because of ongoing face-to-face contact, as well as councils for decision-making in some communities, every member has the opportunity to talk things out, make suggestions, have them heard, and participate in guiding the group. Among the BaMbuti (Pygmy) of the African Congo, interpersonal conflict and offensive acts are settled without any apparent formal mechanism at all. Anyone can discuss any issue that is of concern to the community, and anyone can join in creating solutions. Each dispute is settled as it arises, according to its particular nature, and responsibility for righting the balance is always considered communal.[8] In many nature-based groups, because each person over the age of ten or twelve is capable of surviving in the wilds alone or joining another band, she can leave if she dislikes a decision. A sense of freedom we can hardly fathom reigns: each person can follow his inner guidance or stand up for what he believes, and because of this sense of freedom and responsibility, there is little acting out, rebellion, or addiction to the power games that define politics in mass society.

The atrophy of such freedom appears to be a relatively recent event, a by-product of the emergence of civilization with its propensity for the decidedly undemocratic "heavy stubby legs" of large-scale social organization: expanding population, division of labor, social hierarchy, and centralized governance. In his acclaimed book, *In the Absence of the Sacred*, Jerry Mander reminds us that when European settlers landed on the shores of North America, they brought with them a deep longing for democracy. Having spent their lives within the oppressive monarchies of

Europe, though, they had no experience in starting a democracy
and no hands-on experience in running one. Fortunately for
them, when the Europeans held negotiations with the Indians,
they often did so "in the Indian manner": in democratically run,
consensual councils.[9] In the end, the forefathers of the United
States forged an American constitution, informed by principles
of the Enlightenment and Quakerism, but based essentially on
ways they had learned, heaven forbid, *from hunter-gatherers.*

The idea that democracy is practiced at its best by nature-based
people flies in the face of our perception of these "primitive"
cultures. In particular, it flies in the face of our projections of the
chieftains and medicine men we think run them; in nature-based
communities chiefs are rarely the coercive, authoritarian rulers
we assume them to be. Hierarchy is not particularly developed,
crystallized, or *needed.* In fact, in some groups, like the BaMbuti,
there are no chiefs and no formal councils at all, no juries and no
courts. As nature writer Dolores LaChapelle puts it, "Just as in a
flight of birds turning through the air, no *one* is the leader and
none are the followers, yet all are together."[10]

In communities that do have designated leaders, they are
chosen for the purpose of embodying clan, family, or tribal
heritage. To honor them is not a sign of giving over power; it is an
act of communal self-respect. Leadership may also be situational,
with chiefs chosen for their skills as facilitators and teachers or for
their knowledge of medicine, fishing, or ceremony. The Plains
Indians of North America had literally dozens of chiefs, and
depending on the season or the event, the degree of prominence
accorded to each would shift. No chiefs were ever assured of their
role for a lifetime either; they performed their duties for as long
as they listened well, responded well, and retained full support.
Western people wouldn't necessarily know this, of course, because historically we sought after and valued only the war chiefs.

The anthropologist Francis Huxley tells a marvelous story
about the native relationship to leadership.[11] Because of a medical

emergency, an American friend of Huxley's, also an anthropologist, transported an Indian man from the sweltering wilds of the Xingu Valley in Brazil to the bustling "wilds" of the city of São Paulo. The year was 1955, and what followed was an archetypal moment: Natural Man Meets Modernity. As the two men made their way through the streets among towering buildings, sooty traffic jams, and electric crowds, they passed by a massive bank. Standing erectly at the entrance were two stern security guards, each wearing an elaborate military uniform with black, Gestapo-like boots and carrying a loaded machine gun. The native man was puzzled by this spectacle, never having seen anything like it, and he asked what it might be. Taken aback by the challenge of describing a nation state's economic system to a hunter-gatherer, the American flailed about, stuttered, and scratched his head just as Harwood had. Finally he explained that this place was a "house" where "the chief" kept his "riches." The Indian became even more perplexed. He stuttered, scratched his head, and then declared, "Well then, if he needs *this* much guarding, he cannot be a very good chief."

Dine' Necklace

A third practice common to nature-based cultures is *equality of the sexes*. This is clearly a topic charged with emotion and controversy for us, and many of the addictions we are plagued with—codependence, sexaholism, romance addiction, violence against women—revolve around problematic relations between the sexes. For centuries, probably since the beginning of these painful aberrations of the human experience, women have been addressing their diminished standing in society, calling for greater valuing of their contributions, greater freedom to express themselves, and greater safety in which to lead their lives. It has taken men longer to awaken to the restrictions of the current definitions of manhood, probably because the outward status they are accorded has blinded their insight into the pain and limitations they have been accepting. In the 1970s, though, men have begun realizing and attempting to address, with rage and grief, their need for full humanity.

We might ask if there isn't a deep and universal propensity operating here. If a need for equal opportunity, participation, and rewards were not ingrained in our primal matrix, we might simply accept any definition placed upon us or role assigned to us, no matter how limiting or oppressive. But the raw eruption of discontent in our times tells us that at heart, women and men consist of more than what current social constructs dictate.

Evidence from nature-based cultures reinforces this conclusion. Just as Larry Emerson's turquoise necklace shares different but equal strands for male and female, so the sexes in most nature-based cultures focus on different tasks and modes of expression—while sharing equal opportunity for participation and comparable social status. One detail is worth our notice: perceived differences between women and men may not be as fixed as they have been for us, restrictions not as confining. Women are both nurturing and assertive. They are physically strong, travel the territory with freedom, and have contact with other peoples. Men are intimate with their inner psychic terrains just as they are with the land upon which they hunt, and they participate openly in caring for the children of the band. Probably because of women's biological involvement in childbirth and early child rearing, the main difference in roles is a well-defined division regarding the provision of food—with women gathering plant foods and men hunting animals.

An easy respect between the sexes seems to prevail. Huxley's story about his American anthropologist friend and the Xingu Valley Indian in São Paulo also touches on this issue.[12] To continue: as the two men walked down the street beyond the bank, they passed any number of women slinking by in high heels and tight skirts, carrying overstuffed handbags, their faces plastered with rouge, eye shadow, and lipstick; and the Indian man, again never having witnessed anything like this before, stopped abruptly on the sidewalk. "This is disgusting," he said. "Their faces! Their bodies! Their hips going wrong! Listen," he continued to his American companion, "why don't you just come back to the jungle with me and you can be with my sister, and we won't tell *anybody* about the disgusting things we saw!"

Apart from the grace that Earth-based people emanate through their sexual natures, there is also tremendous freedom in relationship between the sexes. Most relationships in nature-based cultures are entered into by choice and dissolved by choice, rather than rigidly held in place by contracts, conventions, and social pressures. "Commitments are personal, not formal, institutionalized, or rule governed," reports anthropologist Peter Wilson. "Relationships are activated and animated through proximity, and proximity is determined by affection and friendliness."[13] Likewise, ties between spouses are not formal or absolute. To begin, the responsibility for child rearing does not fall heavily onto each isolated nuclear family but is more a communal task. And responsibility for each child does not last twenty years; rather, it lasts no more than six or seven. The upshot is that pressure for women and men to stay locked together in rigid contracts of matrimony does not exist. If they stay together, they do so because they choose to.

Indolent Savages

A fourth social practice common in nature-based cultures concerns *leisure time*. Put another way, there exists in nature-based community a decided absence of workaholism. It seems no coincidence that our modern bodies rebel against the harried work schedules we keep with heart attacks, back problems, cancers, and influenzas that appear so often they are considered "normal." According to a poll taken by Louis Harris and Associates, the average work week in the United States in the 1980s was forty-seven hours, up from forty hours a decade earlier. The U.S. Department of Labor reports that nearly 6 million working men and 1 million working women punch in more than sixty hours a week.[14] (Neither of these statistics includes the extra hours many women, and some men, put in to run their homes and raise their children.)

Journalist Kent MacDougall cuts to the heart of this predicament in a *Los Angeles Times* series entitled "The Harried Society." "Back in 1609 when the Algonkin Indians discovered Henry Hudson sailing up their river," he writes:

> They were living off the fat of the land. They lived so well yet worked so little that the industrious Dutch considered them indolent savages and soon replaced their good life with feudalism. Today, along the Hudson River in New York, supposedly free citizens of the wealthiest society in the history of the world work longer and harder than any Algonkin Indian ever did, race around like rats in a maze, dodging cars, trucks, buses, bicycles, and each other, and dance to a frantic tempo destined to lead many to early deaths from stress and strain.[15]

According to a study conducted by researchers Frederick McCarthy and Margaret McArthur, the average workday for men in aboriginal communities in Western Arnhem Land, Australia, including all time spent on economic activities such as hunting and tool repair, adds up to three hours and forty-five minutes; for women, for their plant collecting and food preparation, the average workday is three hours and fifty minutes.[16] Anthropologist Richard Lee reports that in Africa, the average Dobe Bushman's workweek is fifteen hours, or two hours and nine minutes a day—with only 65 percent of the population working at all. "A woman gathers in one day enough food to feed her family for three days," explains Lee:

> and spends the rest of her time resting in camp, doing embroidery, visiting other camps, or entertaining visitors from other camps. During each day at home, kitchen routines, such as cooking, nut cracking, collecting firewood, and fetching water, occupy one to three hours of her time. This rhythm of steady work and steady leisure is maintained throughout the year. The male hunters tend to work more frequently than the women, but their schedule is uneven. It is not unusual for a man to hunt avidly for a week and then do no hunting at all for two or three weeks. During these periods, visiting, entertaining, and especially dancing are the primary activities of men.[17]

So Many Mongongo Nuts

Another benefit of the nature-based way of life is *good nutrition.* Neurophysiological studies tell us that the chemical imbalances resulting from poor nutritional intake often lay the foundation for, or exacerbate, the psychological imbalances that manifest themselves as substance and behavioral addictions, while over-consumption of foods like sugar and caffeine only adds to this downward spiral. Yet in technological society, we tend to believe that we are magically blessed with endless pyramids of Princess grapefruit, cornucopias of fried chicken, and instant-coffee-under-glass—while Earth-based people exist in a constant state of malnutrition, if not starvation, and a tooth-and-claw struggle for food.

The truth of the matter is that we westerners have lost our ancestral knowledge of how to survive on the Earth. A subterranean fear of not having enough food lies at the base of our civilized psyches, expressed obliquely in personal and cultural messages whose deeper meanings we would rather overlook. Clean your plate! Think of the starving children in China! Cut down the cholesterol! Avoid Alar! Cook from the four food groups! Fast food! I scream for ice cream! In the 1950s, the grand prize of a national contest was three minutes to careen through a supermarket with an empty shopping cart and grab as much food as possible, and the image on our television screens of housewives frantically stuffing turkeys into their wire carts made us all feel exhilarated—and nervous. Anxiety about food is also expressed in epidemic eating disorders like anorexia, bulimia, overeating, and overdieting.

Since Columbus arrived in North America, a full 75 percent of the wildwood ecosystem has been wiped out. Originally, 95 percent of western and central Europe was covered with lush forestland, from the Black Forest to the Italian Alps; that amount is now 20 percent. Ten thousand years ago, China was 70 percent forest; today it is 5 percent.[18] The age-old sense that nature provides has rightfully been lost, and we are rightfully scared to death about our next meal. As Marshall Sahlins reports in his book *Stone Age Economics*, "One-third to one-half of humanity are said to go hungry every night. Some twenty million [are] in the U.S. alone. . . . *This* is the era of unprecedented hunger. *Now*, in the time of greatest technical power, is starvation an institution."[19] Indeed, in the wake of the technology fueled Green Revolution of the 1970s, we have witnessed increasing famine, starvation, the dependence of hundreds of thousands of people on airlifts and feeding camps, a decline in the nutritional quality of all food, and an overall loss of momentum in world food production.

By contrast, true nature-based people rely on a diversity of food sources, and simultaneous failure of all resources is highly unlikely. Anxiety about food is rare, and when it appears, it is usually seasonal. In his book *Health and the Rise of Civilization*, Mark Nathan Cohen reports that food supplies among nature-based people are usually abundant and reliable, while starvation may occur but is rare.[20] Surely there have been times of hardship and uncertainty, but nature-based people who have lived unhampered by the encroachment of civilization tend to hold the attitude that since food is available in abundance, storing it is unnecessary; nature itself stores food for people, who merely need to know how to find it. Pau d'arco. Salmonberry. Wild turkey. Mugwort. Yucca flower. Jamaica ginger. Perhaps the famed statement by an African Dobe Bushman says it all: "Why should we plant when there are so many mongongo nuts in the world?"[21]

Then there is the issue of quality. Anthropologist Peter Farm writes that truly nature-based peoples are "among the best fed people on Earth and also among the healthiest."[22] It goes without saying that those who live in the wilds eat organic food, uncontaminated by chemical preservatives, pesticides, and other additives. Descriptions of the diets of nature-based peoples throughout the world reveal that they uniformly match the standards of the National Research Council of America for consumption of vitamins, minerals, and protein,[23] while erosion of the quality of the nature-based diet consistently occurs when outsiders invade, bring in technological agriculture, cattle, or mining, and set up trade networks and outposts of civilization.

Also, because of their healthy diets, relaxed life-styles, and clean environs, nature-based people do not fall prey to such modern diseases as cancer, coronary heart disease, hypertension, and diabetes. High cholesterol is unknown. Studies of isolated peoples in South America reveal that infectious diseases like influenza, mumps, polio, and smallpox occur but cannot be transmitted in epidemic proportion by small, self-contained groups. Blood pressure is commonly low, and such intestinal disorders as appendicitis, diverticulosis, and bowel cancers are rare—until such groups are introduced to civilized diets.[24] According to the nineteenth-century German physician Samuel

Hahnemann, the founder of homeopathic medicine, the basic "miasms" or energetic patterns of weakness that underlie and prepare the way for modern diseases did not even *exist* in human history until the transition out of nature-based culture.[25]

Contraceptive on Your Hip

A sixth practice common to nature-based cultures is a relatively *stable population.* In today's world the human population is spinning out of control, and along with this explosion of humanity, the capacity of our biosphere to sustain life is being stressed to the breaking point. In 1992 the U.S. National Academy of Sciences and the British Royal Society issued their first joint report, warning: "If current predictions of population growth prove accurate and patterns of human activity on the planet remain unchanged, science and technology may not be able to prevent either irreversible degradation of the environment or continued poverty for much of the world."[26]

As the current global population approaches 6 billion, people everywhere around the world are starving—in "undeveloped" areas like Bangladesh and Nicaragua, in "developing" nations like India and China, in industrial countries like the republics of the former Soviet Union, and on the streets of overdeveloped cities like New York and Los Angeles. Projections from the United Nations Fund for Population Activities estimate that the total human population will grow, before leveling off, to an unfathomable *16 billion.*[27]

According to physicist Vandana Shiva of India, rapid population growth is typical not of secure, sustainable societies but of "displacement, dispossession, alienation of people from their survival base, and inequality of women."[28] As I will discuss in the next chapter, the transition from nomadic foraging to agricultural civilizations constitutes the original "displacement, dispossession, alienation of people from their survival base, and inequality of women." Some ten thousand years ago, when all human societies on the Earth were nature-based, global population was stabilized at 5 million people.[29] According to archaeologist Fekri Hassan, yearly population growth in those times ranged from .01 to .005 percent,[30] while today's world population is exploding with an additional 95 million *each year*.[31]

The ability to maintain numerical stability exists in human history *only* in nature-based cultures. Methods of family planning built into hunter-gatherer life worked successfully for a million years, allowing the human population to grow gradually but not to overrun its capacity to live sustainably. This success is attributable to fertility-control factors that evolved when people lived as nomadic hunter-gatherers—and that disintegrated when civilization emerged or, for many people around the world, was introduced by force.

One of these factors is long-term breast-feeding.[32] As I have mentioned, foraging women carry their children on gathering treks, into rivers, through forests, sitting around the fire, and they feed them on demand for the first three or four years of their young lives. This practice offers yet another facet of the elliptical whole of the natural world: it not only provides the nurturance necessary for the child's physical and psychological development, but can trigger the secretion of a pituitary hormone that suppresses the mother's menstrual cycle. As Lee puts it, the child's frequent stimulation of the breast is "rather like carrying your contraceptive on your hip."[33]

Other contributing factors to low birthrates among nature-based women include a noticeably late onset of menstruation, as well as extended periods when the blood cycle simply disappears.[34] Contemporary researchers attribute these physiological conditions, in part, to the high-protein diets and lean bodies of hunter-gatherer women and, in part, to the strenuous demands of walking long distances while carrying equipment, mounds of

plant food, and children—physical conditions that are repro-
duced among today's female athletes who also report fewer periods and irregular cycles. The upshot of all these factors is that
family size is small, the pressures we typically associate with child
rearing are more relaxed, and population remains low—because
for every woman of reproductive age, a new child arrives but
every five, six, or seven years.

Most of the Trees

A last social quality typical of nature-based life is *ecological sustainability*. This is a quality we want desperately to attain and yet,
for all our Earth Days, eco-conferences, recycling programs, and
environmental regulations, it remains elusive. As we know all too
well, the situation is dire. The kinds of technologies that are
needed to maintain our ever-expanding mass civilization, from
nuclear and chemical to mining and electromagnetic, virtually
encase the planet. Addiction to consumerism, military buildup,
and industrial expansion is so rampant as to be considered normal
by many people and certainly by those who identify with these
developments. Yet, at the same time, scientists studying global
disasters such as climate change, ozone depletion, and toxic
contamination estimate that we have until the year 2000, or
maybe 2010, to turn around the unecological practices that are
causing global destruction.

During the 1980s when I was working to stop the proliferation
of nuclear weapons, I had a disturbing conversation with a corporate CEO. While we were dining one summer evening in a
Hakka restaurant in San Francisco's Chinatown, he told me that
from a business standpoint, nuclear war would not occur until
multinational corporations had succeeded in commercializing
China. After that accomplishment, he said, there would be no

more room on Earth to expand the market economy (which must always, of course, be in a state of expansion), and so there would be no more viable reason for humans beings to stay alive. His opinion reflects the going ethos of both an expansionist technological system and an addicted psyche: use up what resources are here now; when you run out, do whatever you must to get more—with no regard for the consequences.

By contrast, nature-based people neither force the Earth to produce at maximum levels nor impose wholesale realignments of nature's rhythms and physical layout. A commitment to ecological sustainability was the ground upon which our humanity came into existence, and the sustainable life is inseparably intertwined with full participation in social life, democratic decision-making, self-esteem for both women and men, a relaxed approach to daily life, good food, and a stable population. The key seems to be that we humans can successfully survive on this planet only so long as our presence contributes to and meshes with the life of the Earth. According to Marshall Sahlins, within nature-based cultures this objective is accomplished by a gestalt of factors that are its hallmarks: "labor power is underused, technological means are not fully engaged, natural resources are left untapped . . . production is low relative to existing possibilities. The work day is short. The number of days off exceeds the number of work days. Dancing, fishing, games, sleep, and ritual seem to occupy the greater portion of one's time."[35]

Plus, nature-based people move on when existing sources reach their limit, and this limit is never the outer maximum limit of the terrain as we have come to define it. Rather than clear-cut the entire forest, kill every deer, pocket every chestnut, pull up every wild yam, and catch every salmon, nature-based people understand that to let *most* of the trees stand, *most* of the animals run free, *most* of the fruit drop to the ground, *most* of the vegetables complete their cycle, and *most* of the fish swim away is to honor nature's sacred wholeness. As with a Keres word that "doesn't break down into anything," to live this way is to participate in the great round of the natural world; it is to enhance the Earth's abundance and, at the same time, to ensure the sustainability, survivability, and sanity of the human community.

PART TWO

Domestication and Its Discontents

We have forgotten who we are
We have alienated ourselves from the unfolding of the cosmos
We have become estranged from the movements of the earth
We have turned our backs on the cycles of life.
We have forgotten who we are.

—United Nations
Environmental Sabbath
Program

White, European-American, Western peoples are
separated by many generations from decisions of
councils of the whole, small-group nomadic life with
few possessions, highly developed initiation
ceremonies, natural history as everyman's vocation, a
total surround of non-man-made otherness with
spiritual significance, and the 'natural' way of mother
and infant.

—PAUL SHEPARD,
Nature and Madness

4

Original Trauma

You may find yourself
Behind the wheel of a large automobile
And you may find yourself
Living in a beautiful house
With a beautiful wife
And you may ask yourself,
Well, how did I get here?

—TALKING HEADS, "Once in a
Lifetime"

INEAR perspective is a way of seeing things. Things close to us are large, it tells us; things farther away get smaller and smaller as they recede toward a single point in the distance. The vantage point, from slightly above the scene, is that of a "bird's-eye view." Most westerners accept this way of seeing as a complete description of reality. Let's look again. As psychologist Robert Romanyshyn describes this approach in his book *Technology as Symptom and Dream,* seeing life with the mathematical precision of linear perspective means seeing it from a very particular psychological stance: detachment.[1]

In the fifteenth century, when this artistic device was invented, an enormous change in perception was under way in the European mind. The social and technological changes initiated by the domestication process some ten thousand years earlier no longer consisted of the relatively minor alterations of the terrain that had characterized its initial phases. Now farms, villages, and cities were sprouting up; enclosures were resculpting a once-open countryside. These cumulative changes were becoming so all-encompassing to the human experience that they were literally creating a qualitative shift in perception. No longer were people finding themselves *in* the world as vibrant participants touching, feeling, and breathing the richness of its storm clouds and stars; we were beginning to shield ourselves from the natural world, to become spectators of our own lives. No longer were we experiencing events as a round of earthly happenings in which we were embedded; rather, the events of the world were turning into human-constructed exhibitions for our visual entertainment and intellectual commentary. The world itself seemed to be losing the tactile totality we had once known it to have, becoming instead like a "view" from a "window."

Romanyshyn describes linear perspective, with its emphasis on detachment from both the natural world and the human community, as one of the manifest expressions of this change. He illustrates the change by comparing two anonymous paintings of the city of Florence, Italy—one painted before the invention of linear perspective in about 1350; the other after it, in 1480. In the first painting Florence appears as an anarchistic cluster of buildings without any fixed point of view from which to observe them. The art historian Samuel Edgerton writes of this work, "The painter . . . did not conceive of his subject in terms of spatial homogeneity. . . . He could render what he saw before his eyes convincingly by representing what it felt like to walk about, experiencing structures, almost tactilely, from many different sides, rather than from a single, overall vantage." The second painting, called *Map with a Chain*, is more like a photograph, offering a bird's-eye view—a "fixed viewpoint" in Edgerton's words, "elevated and distant, completely out of plastic or sensory reach of the depicted city."[2]

In the centuries to follow, the scientific paradigm emerged, elaborating upon linear perspective and justifying it with a coherent codification of fragmentation, linear casuality, and detachment. During this same stretch of history, four other social developments reflected and reinforced the fact that those people not in sync with the evolving stance of dislocation were to be viewed "completely out of plastic or sensory reach" of the human heart.

The witch-hunts began in the fifteenth century. Eventually hundreds of thousands of people—mostly women, mothers, and healers—would be hanged, drowned, or burned in town squares all across Europe for nothing more than seeing life from the old elliptical, nature-based perspective. The perpetrators of this atrocity were people whose psyches had already become so detached from life's sacred pulse that they were capable of enacting, and rationalizing, mass public murder. At the same time, across the sea, the slaughter of the indigenous peoples of the North American continent was launched, peoples whose blatant participation in the natural world defied the emerging European insistence on alienation. The mental hospital was invented in the seventeenth century. It functioned to shield the public from exposure to people who were capable, in their minds, of achieving nonordinary states of consciousness or, by their behavior, of demonstrating nonordinary realities. Then there was slavery. Although slavery had developed in the west in neolithic times, the brutal importation of African tribespeople to the "new world," also in the seventeenth century, signaled a new magnitude of disjuncture in the western psyche.

By the eighteenth century, when the linear-scientific mind-set had become almost completely solidified as the accepted version of reality, William Wordsworth wrote,

> *Science appears but what in truth she is,*
> *Not as our glory and our absolute boast,*
> *But as a succedaneum, and a prop*
> *To our infirmity.*

The "infirmity" he was describing was a psychospiritual one: *dissociation*—of mind from body, intellect from feeling, human from natural world.

The emergence of this infirmity had been a long time coming, in slow and continual evolution ever since the initiation of a psychic and ecological development some ten thousand years before. This historic development, the launching of the neolithic, was an occurrence that began penetrating the human mind the moment we purposefully isolated domestic plants from natural ones, the moment we captured beasts from their homes in the wild and corralled them into human-built enclosures. Previous to this event humans had indeed participated in the evolution of the natural world—carrying seeds, through the wilderness, dropping, scattering, or planting them, returning later to harvest them; hunting animals by building branch and rock obstructions; catching fish and insects; constructing temporary shelters out of rock, trees, and ice. But this development was something different, something unprecedented. This was the purposeful separation of human existence from the rest of life: the domestication of the human species. To Paul Shepard's mind, the original dualism—the tame/wild dichotomy—came into being, and with it, the elliptical wholeness of the world was clipped.[3]

The fence was the ultimate symbol of this development. What came to reside within its confines—domesticated cereals, cultivated flowers, oxen, permanent housing structures—was said to be tame; to be valued, controlled, and identified with. What existed outside was wild—"weeds," weather, wind, the woods—perennially threatening human survival; to be feared, scorned, and kept at bay. This dichotomy has since crystallized and come to define our lives with the myriads of fences separating us from the wild world and the myriads of fencelike artifacts and practices we have come to accept as "the way things are": economic individualism, private property, exclusive rights, nation-states, resource wars, nuclear missiles—until today our civilization has nearly succeeded at domesticating the entire planet and is looking, in the near future, to enclose both the outer space of other planets and the inner space of our own minds, genes, and molecules.

"Separation," writes feminist philosopher Susan Griffin of this phenomenon. "The clean from the unclean. The decaying, the putrid, the polluted, the fetid, the eroded, waste, defecation, from the unchanging. . . . The errant from the city. The ghetto. The ghetto of Jews. The ghetto of Moors. The quarter of prostitutes. The ghetto of blacks. The neighborhood of lesbians. The prison. The witch house. The underworld. The underground. The sewer. Space divided. The inch. The foot. The mile. The boundary. The border. The nation. The promised land. The chosen ones. The prophets, the elect, the vanguard, the sanctified, the canonized, and the canonizers."[4]

In the psychotherapeutic process, one assumption mental-health professionals consistently make is that whatever behavior, feeling, or state of consciousness a person experiences, expresses, or presents exists for a reason. A good reason. If you and I were given the task of acting as psychotherapists for this domesticated world, we would immediately focus our attention on the "presenting symptom" of separation and divisiveness. We might wonder if the overwhelming success of linear perspective as the sole definition of visual reality isn't a symptom of some deeper condition seeking expression. And we might ask: why did some humans create—and then rationalize with elaborate devices, ideologies, and defenses—an unprecedented way of seeing the world that is based on distancing and detachment?

For a clue, we might look to survivors of post-traumatic stress disorder: Vietnam veterans, rape victims and survivors of childhood abuse, sufferers of both natural and technology induced disasters. One of the most common symptoms to manifest itself after the experience of trauma is the neurophysiological response of disembodiment—"leaving one's body" to escape from pain that is literally too overwhelming to bear. Some people who have endured traumatic events, in describing the experience, tell of a sensation of "lifting out of their bodies," of watching the event from a vantage point slightly above, a vantage point not unlike that of linear perspective. Others tell of escaping into a post-trauma state of mental activity devoid of feeling or body awareness, a state not unlike that considered "normal" in today's dominant culture and taught in our schools and universities.

As psychotherapists, we might eventually wonder and ask: could it be that our very culture splits mind from body, intellect from feeling, because we as individuals are suffering from post-traumatic stress?

Could it be that we as individuals are dissociated because we inhabit a culture that is founded on and perpetrates traumatic stress?

Could it be that the linear perspective that infuses our vision—from our glorification of intellectual distancing to our debunking of the earthier realms of feeling and intuition; to our relentless "lifting" upward with skyscrapers and space shuttles; to the ultimate techno-utopian vision of "downloading" human knowledge into self-perpetuating computers to make embodied life obsolete—that such a perception is the result of some traumatic violation that happened in our human past?

Mythologies describing pre-agricultural times from cultures as divergent as African, Native American, and Hebraic tell of human beings at one time living in balance on the Earth. The western world claims at least five traditions that describe an earlier, better period: the Hebrew Garden of Eden, the Sumerian Dilum, the Iranian Garden of Yima, the Egyptian Tep Zepi, and the Greek Golden Age. Ovid's words in *Metamorphoses* are among the most cited and most revealing:

Penalties and fears there were none, nor were threatening words inscribed on unchanging bronze; nor did the suppliant crowd fear the words of its judge, but they were safe without protectors. Not yet did the pine cut from its mountain tops descend into the flowing waters to visit foreign lands, nor did deep trenches gird the town, nor were there straight trumpets, nor horns of twisted brass, nor helmets, nor swords. Without the use of soldiers the peoples in safety enjoyed their sweet repose. Earth herself, unburdened and untouched by the hoe and unwounded by the ploughshare, gave all things freely.[5]

Most of these mythic legends go on to tell of a "fall" consistently depicted as a lowering of the quality of human character and culture. In recent decades such stories may have appeared to us as quaint allegories, bedtime stories, or the stuff of a good film. But today, from our situs within the psychological and ecological crises of western civilization, these stories become dreams so transparent we barely need to interpret them. According to myths of the Bantu of southern Africa, God was driven away from the Earth *by humanity's insensitivity to nature*. The Yurok of northern California say that at a certain point in history, *people disrupted nature's balance* with their greed. The Biblical story of Eden tells of a great Fall when Adam and Eve *removed themselves from "the Garden"* and came to know evil.

In his work with survivors of post-traumatic stress, psychotherapist and author Terry Kellogg emphasizes the fact that abusive behaviors—whether we direct them toward ourselves, other people, or other species—are not natural to human beings. People enact such behaviors because *something unnatural has happened to them* and they have become damaged.[6] With this important insight in mind, we might consider that the "fall" described in myths around the world was not a preordained event destined to occur in the unfoldment of human consciousness, as some linear-progressive New Age thinkers posit; nor was it the result of what the Bible terms "original sin," which carries with it the onus of fault and blame. We might consider that this historic alteration in our nature, or at least in how we express our nature, came about as the result of *something unnatural that happened to us*.

What could this "something" be?

Because we are creatures who were born to live in vital participation with the natural world, the violation of this participation forms the basis of our *original trauma*. This is the systemic removal of our lives from our previously assumed elliptical participation in nature's world—from the tendrils of earthy textures, the seasons of sun and stars, carrying our babies across rivers, hunting the sacred game, the power of the life force. It is a severance that in the western world was initiated slowly and subtly at first with the domestication of plants and animals, grew in intensity with the emergence of large-scale civilizations, and has developed to pathological proportion with mass technological society—until today you and I can actually live for a week or a month without smelling a tree, witnessing the passage of the moon, or meeting an animal in the wild, much less knowing the spirits of these beings or fathoming the interconnections between their destinies and our own. Original trauma is the disorientation we experience, however consciously or unconsciously, because we do not live in the natural world. It is the psychic displacement, the exile, that is inherent in civilized life. It is our homelessness.

We tend to think of traumatic experience as a singular and dramatic event. An airplane crash. A murder. A street riot. Trauma can also be long lasting and chronic, as it is for the terrorized soldier fighting in an extended war, a child whose developing years are marred by repeated emotional chaos—or the member of western civilization whose connection to the natural world is damaged by the social and psychic dislocations of domestication. As sociologist Kai Erikson describes it, "A chronic disaster is one that gathers force slowly and insidiously, creeping around one's defenses rather than smashing through them."[7]

The negative effects of trauma are often passed from person to person, generation to generation, people to people, culture to culture. When the traumatic experience is left unhealed and dissociated from consciousness, traumatized people can reenact their pain by unconsciously performing aberrant or abusive behaviors that then affect their children and so on down through the generations, or that affect other people and so on down through history. This ongoing pattern is the cycle of abuse so well known in the addiction/recovery community; it is the history-repeats-itself syndrome of our collective life.

My discovery of childhood abuse was a turning point in my understanding of this intergenerational inheritance. I had been plagued by a feeling of horror and terror that appeared, in my mind's eye, as a giant thistle scratching against the insides of my belly. Finally so exasperated that I could no longer bear the discomfort, I decided to remove the thistle from my abdomen and unpeel it. As I did this, to my utter shock, a vision floated into view, at first wispy like a trail of smoke, and then clear and stark and unmistakable: my father was lying on a bed naked, his penis red like a piece of meat and erect, and a child lay next to him, face down, paralyzed in horror and terror. The next day my body involuntarily enacted the experience of being raped, but this time with the response I had been unable to muster as the child threatened with death if I called for help, told, or even remembered: I kicked at my father's huge body, flipped away from his assault, and screamed with all my might for my mother.

As these events sprang from their forty-year cover of amnesia into the consciousness of a summer day, I realized that my father had probably also been abused—if not sexually, in some other enduring way. I was able to document an unyielding strain of alcoholism and the twistings of mental illness throughout the family line, and I surmised that the pain of abuse, in one form or another, reached back to the generation before his and to the one before that and before that and before that. Healing, I realized, would engage me in a process greater than that of addressing the trauma in my own body and psyche. If I could heal myself of the traumatic violations of my own childhood, I would in effect be healing *and stopping* the suffering of an entire lineage—of my father and his father before him, of his grandmother and her mother before her—reaching all the way back three hundred generations to the original trauma that had catalyzed all this pain: our separation from the Earth.

Others have investigated similar perspectives. Sigmund Freud wrote his infamous *Civilization and Its Discontents* late in life, after he had had a lifetime to test the effectiveness of his psychoanalytic system. In this book Freud unveils three jarring ideas that were decidedly unpopular amid the fear and chaos of pre–World War II Europe, and remain so today: (1) ultimately it is civilization itself, not the innate drama of the human psyche, that disrupts the true nature of people; (2) the miseries, crimes, and conflicts so rampant in society are obvious symptoms of this unnatural re-working of the psyche; and (3) the psychoanalytic approach, or any individualized approach to psychological healing, may in the larger scheme of things offer no more than superficial relief.[8]

Physician Samuel Hahnemann had explored similar territory a century earlier. As I have already mentioned, Hahnemann traced the diseases plaguing people in the nineteenth century back to several "miasms," or basic energetic patterns of weakness. In *The Chronic Diseases*, a book also written from the perspective of later life, Hahnemann describes these miasms as the accumulated collective diseases of humanity, traceable to the formation of civilization and our simultaneous dislocation from the natural world.[9] The implication of this view is that for us to heal ourselves of current physical and psychological illness, we must address not just the weaknesses that have resulted from events in our own individual lives; we must address these deeper, chronic, collective imbalances as they appear in each one of us and in our way of life.

In a similar vein, eco-feminist philosophers Starhawk and

Johanna Maybury define repeated atrocities such as war, violence, and oppression as systemic social dysfunctions, tracing their current manifesations back to historical traumas that both spring from previous collective and personal abuses and also prepare the way for subsequent collective and personal abuses.[10] For European peoples, one of the most dramatic of these historic traumas is the witch-hunts of the fifteenth, sixteenth, and seventeenth centuries, events that directly affected the lives of nine generations and indirectly all of their descendants. From this perspective, could my suffering as a victim of childhood abuse actually trace back to the suffering expressed and catalyzed during the Inquisition? According to Maybury, any successful attempt made by people of European ancestry to heal must, of course, address individual dysfunctions caused by directly experienced trauma—and also the psychic legacy of historic upheavals, like the witch-hunts, in our shared psychology.

Indeed, there are moments in history when the cumulative trauma coursing through the human psyche can no longer be contained within the individual, erupting in some collective horror. At Aacqu (Acoma) in northern New Mexico, Spanish conquistadors chopped off the hands of the Indians inhabiting the mesa pueblo and threw the bodies of young warriors, women, children, and elders over the side of the cliff. From 1934 to 1953, Joseph Stalin's purges against the Soviet citizenry killed 10 million people. Twenty-seven million Soviets died in World War II. Nazi Germany's Holocaust slaughtered 17 million. Are you taking this in? In the 1950s, Chinese soldiers, some of them no older than teenagers, stormed into mountain monasteries in Tibet to bludgeon the monks who, minutes before, had been chanting and meditating. Since the Vietnam War three times as many U.S. soldiers have killed themselves by their own traumatized hands as died in combat.

Historic events like these are sobering indeed. Yet they are different only in scale from individual acts that are interwoven throughout everyday life in our civilization, acts ranging from abduction along a medieval roadside to mass murder in a 1990s trailer court, and practices deemed socially acceptable for millenia, like men in classical Greece routinely using young boys for sex or today's parents disciplining their children with violence.

As we trace the interplay of personal and collective dysfunction back through the generations, all kinds of questions arise—specific questions like: what part did alcohol abuse play in the colonization of the North American continent? If a Euro-American man was engaged in killing Indian people or enslaving Africans, what could his relationship with his children have been like? How did German family relations pave the way for the Holocaust? What impact did the Holocaust have on German family relations? On Jewish family relations?

Ultimately specific psychohistorical questions like these lead us to another, more fundamental, perhaps more crucial question. How did this vast cycle of personal and collective pathology begin?

5

Domestication

Saddle, yoke: man becomes a beast of burden.

—ANDREW SCHMOOKLER,
The Parable of the Tribes

THE cycle of pathology as we know it begins with domestication. What could be more peaceful than a farm with rows of corn? you may ask. Or more healthy than a ranch with a herd of cattle? According to biologist James Lovelock, "By far the greatest damage we do to the Earth, and thus by far the greatest threat to our survival, comes from agriculture."[1] Anthropologists Lionel Tiger and Robin Fox have called agriculture "the great leap backward,"[2] while physiologist Jared Diamond of UCLA Medical School has declared it to be "the worst mistake in the history of the human race."[3] To its critics, the pastoral way of life fares no better. Cultural philosopher Charlene Spretnak faults its warrior-hero mentality and patriarchal monotheism.[4] To Paul Shepard, the emergence of animal breeding constitutes psychohistorical "regression."[5] As innocent as they may appear, agriculture and pastoralism as sources of human livelihood have proven devastating to human psyche, society, and the Earth.

No one fully understands why people began to control and manage the natural world by cultivating wild plants and taming wild animals.[6] The most popular theory is a geo-anthropological one, positing that global climatic change some ten thousand years ago altered growing patterns all over the world and forced people to improvise more consciously managed livelihoods. Another school of thought suggests that people became sedentary first, and that fenced planting and animal husbandry naturally followed suit. A third proposes a radical increase in population, demanding the development of radically increased food sources. A fourth theory points to the hunter-gatherer practice of "budding off" to start new bands, resulting ultimately in the impingement of one group upon another.

Whatever the origins of these unprecedented livelihoods, nature-based people throughout the Near East, southeastern Europe, and Eurasia altered a millenia-old way of active, respectful participation with nature's ways by supplementing their age-old sources of wild food with consciously planted grains and legumes and captured sheep. At first the change was relatively minor, with early domesticates representing no more than 5 percent of the total diet.[7] In time, though—because of internal pressures inherent in the change—the ways of domestication took precedence and, according to Shepard, "the domestication of plants and animals led to a Neolithic dialectic, a split in husbandry between pastorality and tillage. . . . What to their ancestral hunter-gatherers had been a polar equilibrium whereby men hunted and women gathered was sundered into masculinist and patriarchal societies of animal breeders on the one hand and Great Mother–worshipping, plant-tending cultivators of the soil on the other."[8] Eventually, these new ways spread throughout the region, sometimes by diffusion, sometimes by force, laying the foundation for what became western civilization.

The effects of this transition were more profound than any that had yet, or have since, taken place. The small-scale, nomadic life that had endured through more than a million years and thirty-five thousand generations was irreparably altered. The human relationship to the natural world was gradually changed from one of respect for and participation in its elliptical wholeness to one of detachment, management, control, and finally domination. The social, cultural, and ecological foundations that had previously served the development of a healthy primal matrix were undermined, and the human psyche came to develop and maintain itself in a state of chronic traumatic stress.

Such a phenomenon is difficult to describe. As educator Raymond Williams writes, "The problem of the knowable community is . . . a problem of language,"[9] and surely we have no adequate language to give account to this development and its effects on the human community. To begin, the words we must use have their roots in the very severance we are attempting to name. As historian Calvin Martin puts it, "I don't have the language to truly convey the richness of what my still-paleolithic mind senses. . . . I speak the language of the neolithic, the triumphant tongue of man apart, the voice of history."[10] Cheyenne-Hodulee Muscogee activist Suzan Harjo tells me that there are no words in Native American languages to describe the scope of suffering and dislocation that the European inheritors of this chronic traumatic stress perpetrated upon Indian people.[11] Robert Jay Lifton reports that survivors of Hiroshima insist that no words are powerful enough to help them understand, or accept, what happened to them.[12]

And yet, at least to speak of the trauma and its effects, using the language that trauma has bequeathed may be the only verbal means we have. Psychiatrist Chaim Shatan makes a stab, calling the rupture that brings people to enact destruction and abuse "man-made stress and unhealed psychic reality."[13] Freud wrote of the phenomenon: "Men have gained control over the forces of nature to such an extent that with their help they would have no difficulty in exterminating one another to the last man. They know this, and hence comes a large part of their current unrest, their unhappiness and their mood of anxiety."[14] Lifton calls this rupture "the broken connection."[15] I call it original trauma. None of these words begins to capture its meaning.

How it happened is a story that brings us to the interconnectedness of all things, from sexuality and food production to
community and our relationship to the Earth—but from a standpoint not of the health and harmony we typically use to concep-
tualize interconnectedness, but of dysfunction.

Many feminists today are quick to blame the dysfunction on a
succession of violent invasions by Indo-European pastoralists in
the latter neolithic. The extent of these invasions is debated.
Researchers such as Marija Gimbutas, Riane Eisler, and Merlin
Stone highlight their abrupt introduction of hierarchy, weap-
onry, and monotheism as *the* turning point of western history.[16]
Researchers like Colin Renfrew question the magnitude of
their impact,[17] while most anthropological texts treat them as
no more or less important than other recurring expansions,
invasions, social collapses, and disasters common to the period.
While emotions on the issue run hot, the most frequently
overlooked facet of the exploration is the inherent potential
within even the earliest efforts at organized planting for many of
the same pitfalls found in the more obviously violent pastoral
society. From this perspective, the ultimate problem seems not
to be one of agriculture versus pastoralism—but one of domestication itself.

Seeds of Change

The most obvious change that took place during the transition to
a livelihood based on planting was the fact that, in order to tend
the plots of land, people eventually had to settle in one place all
year round. For the first time in all of history, people began to
build substantial housing and storage structures and to accumu-
late more possessions than they could carry on their backs.[18]
According to many commentators who have researched the
ramifications of this transition, seeds of grain were not the only

things planted; the seeds of private property and class stratification were also sown.[19]

The British anthropologist Margaret Ehrenberg describes this sowing in her book *Women in Prehistory*. "The development of agriculture brought with it a large increase . . . in the range of material possessions such as farming and food-preparation tools and storage vessels," she writes.

> On the one hand, this may be seen as the spur to the development of craft specialisation, as some individuals concentrated on the production of one particular item, which they would exchange for other products or services. . . . Increasingly some people might have found that they could acquire enough food and other necessities by producing only one specialised article. . . . These material possessions, as well as the domesticated animals themselves, would have constituted considerable wealth, which could be accumulated and handed on from one generation to the next. . . . As one family accumulated more cattle, or acquired better ploughs, or were able to exchange more goods because of their specialized craft skills, the gap between their wealth and that of their neighbors would increase progressively. . . . A distinction between rich and poor, which is insignificant in forager societies, develops progressively as wealth is passed on from generation to generation within some families, while others are never able to achieve surpluses. . . . The wealthy become powerful by lending to poorer families in return for services, such as farm labour, or support in combat against other groups. By this means the rich are able to become more wealthy, while the poor become indebted to other families, and have to produce more and more, or spend time on tasks other than directly for their own subsistence. So the vicious circle develops.[20]

As I have already mentioned, the size of the nature-based band had been maintained by fertility-control factors built into life in the wilds. The initiation of a livelihood based on conscious planting began to disrupt these factors—and women began to have more babies than ever before. According to archaeological evidence, the spread of sedentary communities in the Near East brought with it a 700 percent population increase,[21] and as anthropologist Donald O. Henry sees it, sedentism itself is what caused this explosion.[22]

To begin, the kind of work required of women for the prepa- ration, maintenance, and harvesting of cultivated land was more demanding and mechanistic than the fluid, integrated work of the gatherer. As a result, carrying a child on one's hip became truly burdensome, and since life was now lived in one place, children could easily be contained within pens or special rooms built for this very purpose. As time passed, women also discon- tinued the lengthy periods of breast-feeding that had previously lasted for the first three or four years of their babies' lives because the demands of planting began to overwhelm their time and attention;[23] the contraceptive-on-your-hip was eventually lost, and postpartum ovulation returned sooner than it ever had before.

Other fertility-control factors were also lost with the advance of organized planting. The high-protein diet of the hunter- gatherer gave way to a high-carbohydrate diet whose centerpiece was the now-available domesticated grains. Women became less lean, storing more fat on their bodies and so ovulating with more regularity. Soft-grain cereal provided an obvious baby-food sub- stitute for mother's milk, contributing to the move to briefer periods of breast-feeding and earlier postpartum ovulation.[24] The new sedentary lifestyle also encouraged women to become less active than they had been, a change that also contributed to the new regularity of ovulation.[25] What resulted from this gestalt of personal and social changes were more babies born more often, perhaps as often as one each year for every woman of childbearing age; the bands of hunter-gatherers with their small families were, through time, expanding into the large farming family with eight to ten children. To the certain surprise and probable dismay of everyone, the population explosion, however humble its beginnings, was on.

Work was also becoming more tedious and stressful. As time passed, everyone had to work harder and longer to maintain a system of food production whose goal was to serve an ever-growing community constantly demanding ever more food. Life was changing from a low-key effort with a workweek of maybe fifteen or twenty hours to a going concern of combined planting, foraging, hunting, and fishing that eventually, because of inherent pressures, gave way to a complex mechanistic operation whose maintenance threatened to become a full-time occupation for everyone.[26] The rat race was on.

So was economic expansionism. Women who had previously spent their days trekking over the countryside, climbing trees, and digging up wild yams with a stick were increasingly staying in one place and using that stick to plant seeds. In the first generations of the change, they foraged for food as well as cared for a garden at the campsite. As generations passed, though, the surrounding land, now picked over as never before, came to yield less. Tied to their plots of land for survival, they could no longer break camp, and so, returning again and again to the same forests and meadows for foraging and hunting and to the same acreage for planting, neolithic peoples became the first perpetrators of overuse. Propelled as well by the needs of an increasing population, they began to expand the size of those original gardens.[27] The growth economy was born.

So were resource wars, colonization, and institutionalized defense, posits anthropologist Robert Carneiro,[28] particularly in fertile planting areas locked in by deserts, ocean, or mountains. Since early farming peoples could not solve overpopulation and overuse by moving, they often attempted agricultural intensification, building terraces and irrigation canals and domesticating more plants. But ultimately such measures did not keep pace with the growing needs for food—and so neolithic people turned to warfare, attacking the weakest adjacent village and expropriating its land, harvests, and population.

The need to quantify and standardize things, events, and people arose simultaneously with population growth, economic expansionism, and the taking of vanquished peoples, and herein we find the roots of the transition from the ellipticism of nature-based life to the mechanization of technological society. I became aware of the workings of this phenomenon in the town where I live in northern New Mexico. We have a village market, a restaurant, and a post office. The dusty parking lot of the post office is a testament to well-practiced anarchy. Cars and trucks are parked every which way, with the pattern changing every three or four minutes. Every now and again a horse rider arrives and ties her horse to the flagpole. Dogs lie across the entrance door, people stand around the lobby exchanging stories, and the postmaster smokes a cigarette by the mail slot. The setup works. It is also a fine glimpse into the kind of personal independence and spontaneity that naturally occur in small-scale community and that our nature-based ancestors knew as a matter of course.

I came to see the urge to quantification by the changes taking place in New Mexico. The population in these parts is growing very fast now. Ranches are being subdivided. Developments are booming. People from all over the United States have dubbed the Southwest the last frontier of sanity and are flocking to our town. Their appearance is driving up real-estate prices, using up the last drops of water in the aquifer, tainting the air with exhaust—and threatening to change our ways at the post office. I can imagine the day when parking in whichever-way-works will no longer work. There will be a tarred surface with painted rows and lines telling each "postal consumer" exactly where to park and for how long.[29] Mechanistic thinking, it seems, developed to solve the organizational complexities initiated by population growth.

What happened to our relationship to tools during the transition from a nature-based life to agriculture is of particular interest to us since we now live in a society wholly defined, sustained, and encased by technology. Our tools came to be something other than the homemade, finely crafted artifacts, bowls, spears, and backpacks they had been in the past. New technologies were constantly needed to solve the problems arising from what was becoming an unending spiral of expansion of settlement, increasing complexity, and speeding up of life.[30] The plow was invented to farm the expanding croplands. Grain stores were needed for keeping excess food. Stone querns were needed for grinding grain into flour. Wooden vessels were made for storing cereals in the house. Aqueducts were constructed to transport water for irrigation and human use. People themselves came to be technologized, for the first time in history providing narrowly specific functions to facilitate the process toward growth, complexity, and further mechanization. There were owners to amass the capital required to pursue grander technological projects, managers to oversee the process, priests and priestesses to curb the encroaching alienation and fear.

Each change that came about fostered the need for some personal adjustment, some social reaction, some technological invention that would ease the impact of, or solve the problem caused by, the last adjustment, reaction, or invention. With the increasing grandiosity of human endeavor, the logical development was toward efficiency, standardization, and mechanization that, generations later, would reach full expression in the Industrial Revolution. Because the tools and methods invented did indeed address these growing problems of survival, at least temporarily, we came to regard them as numinous, all-powerful, God-like. The tragedy inherent in this process is that there was seemingly no way to turn it around. As the population grew, as nearly everyone became dependent on a system of increasing domesticated production and technological innovation, as the overused terrain became more and more fragile—there seemed no way out, except to solve each emerging problem with the next fix.

A dysfunctional relationship with the Earth was set in motion as well. (Are you getting overwhelmed?) People had to chop down more trees to clear the land for more crops and provide wood for more houses, furniture, tools, stoves, and fences. Nature's process of recycling nutrients was disrupted by erosion and soil depletion. To create a new system of recycled nutrients for planting, people had to intervene by bringing in artificial inputs like fertilizers, compost, topsoil, redirected water—and more new technologies to make these massive projects workable.

You and I tend to think that excesses associated with agriculture like topsoil depletion and desertification have become seriously problematic only in recent years. Yet take the farming villages of the neolithic—the much-admired Catal Hüyük, for example: wholly abandoned after only twelve hundred years, not because of marauding invaders (who arrived in the area at least one thousand years later) but most probably for its inability to match growing demands for food production with ecological fact.[31] Take the later agricultural civilizations of Sumer, the Mayan world, and Greece. These societies grew directly out of the same events and forces set in motion by the domestication process exemplified at Catal Hüyük. Admittedly, they have inspired classicists, New Age enthusiasts, and psychologists by their elaborate mathematical computations, systems of astronomy, and mythological symbology, and yet archaeological research tells us that they survived through difficult times not by astrological prediction or praying to the gods—but by unflagging agricultural expansion, urban development, and imperialism.

Sumer was peaking as an agricultural civilization in 3500 BC. As the limit of arable land was reached and irrigation caused the soil to become too salty for cultivation, food production fell. By 2000 BC, there were reports of "earth turned white," a clear reference to salinization. By 1700 BC, food production had declined by 65 percent. The Mayan empire grew to include some 5 million citizens (about the size of Los Angeles), but the needs of its vast urban population outgrew the production capacity of the lowland jungle of Central America. People starved and fled, and the deserted fields and cities were lost to the dense overgrowth, only to be found again in the nineteenth century. In ancient Greece, a continually rising population caused farmers to strip bare the ancient hills of Attica within a few generations. Eventually, every one of these civilizations deteriorated into an unihabitable ecological disaster area.[32]

Perhaps saddest of all the effects caused by domestication concerns women and men: their identities, roles, and relationships became tragically distorted. This perversion unfolded in both farming and pastoral societies as men took over responsibility for all food production while women lost the ability to contribute directly to survival.

Among agriculturalists, the change hinged on the role of animals.[33] Sheep domestication emerged some ten thousand years ago in the Jordan Valley. Domesticated goats and sheep appeared throughout southwest Asia and southern Europe about eight thousand years ago, while domesticated cattle were being herded in Turkey by 5800 BC.[34] The job of capturing the herds naturally fell to the still-active hunters. At first, the herds were kept for their meat. It has been proposed that somewhere along the line, someone realized that animals could be harnessed to plow the fields, which were growing too unwieldy for the women to tend.[35] Since this act brought the production of animal and plant foods into a single domain (and because women were simultaneously becoming unduly preoccupied with child rearing), men took over the lion's share of responsibility for the production of both plant and animal foods.

The effort to produce food, previously shared by both sexes, now became solely "a man's world." The men, who had been the hunters, now became breadwinners as well, responsible for *all* food production—not ennobled by their new dual roles, but rather overburdened as they struggled to meet the overwhelming demands placed upon them.

Eco-feminist Adele Getty proposes another development that had profound implications for the male psyche.[36] In captivity, she writes, male animals proved to be too wild and uncontrollable; the use of the word *break* to describe the domestication process is revealing. To answer the problems of this unforeseen predicament, the men sliced off the animals' male organs. In their primal role as hunters, though, men had always revered, communicated with, and identified with the animals they were hunting. As Shepard puts it, the "animals were seen as belonging to their own nation and to be the bearers of messages and gifts of meat from a sacred domain."[37] The brutal act of castration had to have a dramatic impact on the male psyche. The reverberations of this impact are visible even today in Freud's castration anxiety and are unconsciously reenacted again and again, as traumatic themes so often are, in the religiomedical procedure of circumcision, in rape, in sadomasochistic acts, and in sexual violence.

We know less about the development of male-dominated pastoralism because pastoralists left behind little archaeological evidence. We do know that pastoralism came into existence in the same general period as early farming,[38] evolving not in fertile lands, where herding intertwined with sedentary cultivation— but in less productive terrain like the deserts of Egypt and the steppes of western Asia, where people relied more heavily on animals for food. One thing about these societies is certain: like their agricultural brothers, pastoral men took control of food production by breaking the animals, and in so doing they traumatized themselves.

Meanwhile, women maintained relative status and control as long as they were involved in planting, but as soon as men took over food production, they lost both.[39] As we know, the sedentism of agriculture caused women to have more babies. This development was stressful in itself, putting untoward demands on their time and probably contributing to their departure from food production into the secondary "domestic" role. As Ehrenberg describes the change, "The discovery of agriculture, which at the beginning of the neolithic had been such a positive step by women, was by the end of the period to have had unforeseen, and unfortunate, consequences for them."[40] In their new position, women began to do work only indirectly connected to survival activity, such as cooking, making household items, and producing future generations of farm laborers (preferably boys, because male work more directly served survival and was therefore considered more valuable). Women in pastoral societies also lost status and control, only to become "ornaments" and status symbols for their husbands and fathers.[41]

The tragedy is painfully clear: for over 99 percent of human existence, women's role had been absolutely vital for community survival. Now what women did was becoming "women's work," and in this lesser role, they were coming to be economically dependent, incapable of self-sufficiency—and vulnerable as the perfect targets for the mounting rage and terror men were feeling.

Something Unnatural

Can you see what was beginning to happen? An entirely unprecedented way of life arose out of that initial act of severing the human world from the wild. For all the excitement that accompanied this new way of life, for all the grandiosity describing it as the greatest advance toward human achievement, for all the rationalizations hailing it as "progress" and "evolution"—the tame/wild dichotomy actually initiated a spiral of massive social, cultural, economic, and ecological disruption.

According to the third edition of the psychiatric diagnostic text *Diagnostic and Statistical Manual of Mental Disorders*, trauma is defined as "an event that is outside the range of usual human experience and that would be markedly distressing to almost anyone."[42] What could be more "outside the range of usual human experience" than a complete disruption of every single facet of life? What could be more "distressing" than finding ourselves, out of short-term needs, locked into a cycle of abuse that insists we slash, dig, and burn the very Earth we have always respected and known ourselves to be made of? Prop up men fast losing their dignity to an insatiable work machine? Debase and dominate the ancient strength and ingenuity of women? And treat all living beings as cogs in a machine, competitors in a race, or lifeless objects of production?

In the vernacular of the field of post-traumatic stress, *something unnatural was happening to us.*

6

Discontents

How much of the great poetry
of solitude in the woods is one
long cadenza of the sadness

of civilization

—William Matthews,
"Civilization and Its Discontents"

THIS "something unnatural" I have been describing was not just the physical fact that humans were coming to live behind the enclosure of fences, in shut rooms, by the hand of the mechanical clock. It did not happen solely on the external levels of family size, social organization, work load, technological development, and sex roles. This "something unnatural" was also an inner experience, a sense of exile that grew in our souls as we departed from the wilds and came to inhabit a human-contrived world. Calvin Martin describes it as "a breakthrough, more in the sense of rupture, of the human imagination."[1]

Loss of context was the primary contributor to this transition. Uprooted from our place in the natural world, removed from the cycles of sun, star, and season, separated from the creatures who had previously been our friends and teachers, we became homeless. In ways hardly detectable at first, our physical reality grew to be less wild and, with the development of farms, villages, towns, cities, and then megalopolises, artificial. As we increasingly cast ourselves in the role of domesticator of nature, we came to feel not more powerful and in control, but more lost and terrified. No matter what rationale we designed to explain these developments, the fact remained: humans originally evolved in synchronicity with a world made of fireflies, fire ants, and snow clouds. The swirling pattern on the tips of our fingers had been shaped in consonance with the wind, and our cycles of creativity had come to mirror those of the moon. For all the supremacy touted by civilization's surging advocates, the disappearance of our natural home produced a shock whose effects were so comprehensive as to be nearly unspeakable.

Mental Pathology for the Millions

One of these lost psychic qualities was the sense of belonging originally built into our psychic reality by a full personal and cultural relationship with nature, beginning in infancy with the physical contact that the hunter-gatherer life had afforded. Using Erik Erikson's stages of psychosocial development to reveal the losses perpetrated through the evolution of civilization, Paul Shepard points out that loss of intimacy with the natural world went hand in hand with loss of intimacy with one's parents, and specifically, one's mother. "Civilization increased the separation between the individual and the natural world as it did the child from the mother,"[2] he notes, concluding that a growing sense of childhood abandonment produced more insecure adults whose unconsciously driven raison d'être became to act out their unmet needs.

Simon Ortiz, a Keres Indian man from Aacqu, cuts to the core of this insecurity and the intergenerational process stemming from it in a single poem.[3] Reading this poem startled me. In just twenty-five lines Ortiz captures much of what I am trying to say in this book. The poem concerns a prevalent Native American response to colonization, yet its message is equally applicable to the effects of domestication on westernized people.

Somehow
it was impossible
for them
to understand true safety.

Knowledge for them
was impossible
to understand as pain.
That was untrustworthy,
lost to memory.

Death was sin.

Their children
hunkered down, frightened
into quilts, listening
to wind
speaking Arapaho words
for pain and beauty and generations.

But they refused to understand.
Instead, they protested
the northwind,
kept adding rooms.
Built fences.
Their children learned to plan.
Their parents required submission.

Warriors could have passed
into their young blood.

At best, the newly domesticated adults were withdrawn and because of the demands of both livelihood and their weakened psychological state, incapable of nurturing their children's full need for love and support; at worst, they violated their children with disguised retaliation and displaced acts of violence. Increasing numbers of this next generation then grew to be wounded and insecure. Here the internal workings of the cycle of dysfunction are revealed, and the practices we are all too familiar with, from emotional neglect to physical abuse, begin a historical cycle of humans mistreating humans ad nauseam. The cycle of violation against the Earth synchronistically arose, emanating from the new requirements for livelihood as from well as this growing sense of abandonment and rage.

The process of domestication also truncated the development of a sense of personal centeredness. This breach occurred in part because of the initial loss of satisfaction of the need for security; in part because of the growing incidence of intergenerational abuse, a practice that invariably disrupts personal integrity in those who experience it; in part because of the division of reality into tame and wild and the resulting do's and don'ts curtailing personal freedom.

Our ancestors also lost their sense of personal definition because of the demise of human life lived in the wilds. As the wilderness came to be divided up and sculpted for human use, people lost the very context that had originally served the development of personal integrity. Our world became decreasingly organic and wild, increasingly human constructed and technology determined. Since we identified all the technologies, buildings, and roads surrounding us as achievements of the human mind, we forfeited access to the age-old understanding of where each of us begins; instead we came to be locked into an enmeshed, codependent stage of perception in which every single thing—whether mother, car, football team, microscope, or nuclear warhead—" 'R' Us."

Also lost with the advance of civilization was our long-standing ability to enter into nature-induced nonordinary states of consciousness for the purpose of healing, revelation, and connectedness with the natural world. With ever-decreasing contact with the birds, animals, and seasons, we had less opportunity to work out our inevitable psychological conflicts by communion with natural forces. Over the generations we came to forget the healing process with its mysterious unfolding of experience and essence, and this ancient knowledge lost its place at the center of human culture. Instead we increasingly came to view psychological and physical imbalances in the same way we were coming to perceive all the other external problems in our midst—as solvable only by knee-jerk technological fixes like synthetic pills, by mechanistic forms of social control like behavior modification and mental institutions, and by wholesale eradications with shock therapy and lobotomies.

Not surprisingly, as the human psyche came to lose trust, integrity, and communion, as intergenerational abuse became more commonplace, and as the inevitable injuries of an increasingly technological world added to overall stress, the task of healing grew into something more complex than it had ever been. Previously an injured or nightmare-ridden person might visit a medicine woman once or twice, enter into ceremony for a moon, or take an infusion of plant medicine. But now the experience of trauma was becoming all too commonplace— until today when we live almost entirely apart from natural rhythms, encased almost entirely in technological environments and mechanistic social forms, subject to an entire system caught in a seemingly unending cycle of abuse. As the aftershocks of our collective trauma have become "normal" fare for our psyches, healing ourselves has become a lifelong task. Any one of us, you or I, may be harboring the psychic burdens of alcoholic parents, childhood violence, the loss of a sibling, combat service, divorce, rape, illness, drug-addicted children, *plus* robberies, muggings, and car accidents. Add to these the constant violence of racism and sexism, the constant threat of murder in the streets, the unrelenting demise of the ecosphere. Chernobyl. Desert Storm. Bosnia. South Africa.

Given this horrific situation, it is not trauma that has come to exist "outside the range of usual human experience." The traumatizing process is constant and chronic in mass technological society; it is our knowledge of healing and the means to heal from the onslaught that have become nearly lost.

The notion that the post–hunter-gatherer primal matrix exists in a chronic state of traumatic stress may strike many readers as shocking, extreme, or too ominous to consider. This is certainly a perspective that goes against our sunny ethic of progress, which insists we are consistently growing smarter, stronger, healthier, and more evolved. As a lifelong participant in a civilization marked by wanton ecological destruction and endemic psychological tendencies toward abuse and addiction, I have come to question the cynical assumption that such contemporary behaviors are "normal" expressions of "human nature." Native and indigenous peoples have long wondered at the western way of being and seen it as, if not pathological, bizarre. Choctaw-Cree writer Gerald Haslam describes this way of being in a short story, "Hawk's Flight: An American Fable," about a young Indian about to be murdered by white soldiers. He writes: "Hawk found himself feeling a strange kind of pity for these hopeless creatures who possessed no magic at all, no union with Earth or sky, only the ability to hurt and kill   They were sad and dangerous like a broken rattlesnake."[4]

Apart from the largely unrecorded commentary on the western personality made by indigenous people, and enshrined in their humor, Sigmund Freud was one of the first to raise the possibility that civilization itself may be psychopathological. "May we not be justified in reaching the diagnosis that, under the influence of cultural urges," he wrote in 1939, "some civilizations or some epochs of civilization—possibly the whole of mankind—have become neurotic?"[5] Social philosopher Lewis Mumford spoke of "mad rationality,"[6] while the renegade Freudian R. D. Laing asserted that our "socially shared hallucinations, our collusive madness is what we call sanity."[7] Continuing this line of thinking, the psychoanalyst Erich Fromm succinctly observed, "That millions of people share the same form of mental pathology does not make those people sane."[8]

Like a Broken Rattlesnake

Whether manifest in the person or in the collective, trauma has distinct and identifiable psychological symptoms. As psychiatrist Abram Kardiner describes these, "The subject acts as if the original traumatic situation were still in existence and engages in protective devices which failed on the original occasion."[9] Among these devices, we find the following:

Hyperreactivity. This is the chronic anxiety, jumpiness, tendency to knee-jerk reactions, even paranoia of the traumatized individual. Here we have the rape victim looking over her shoulder for the next attacker, the Vietnam veteran breaking out in a cold sweat in a park on a Sunday afternoon. After the 1972 Buffalo Creek flood in West Virginia, one survivor reported: "When I'm at home, I have an urgent need to leave. When I'm away, I have an urgent need to come here. It's like I'm always waiting and watching for something terrible to come along."[10]

This same state of hypervigilence motivates many of our behaviors in collective life. Why are so many men so quick to use violence against women? Think of the knee-jerk rush to sue neighbors and fellow citizens. Or the assumption that any person walking into a store is a potential thief or that all African-American males are hooligans. How about our obsession with "independence" in the form of automotive mobility? Or how we keep our gas tanks full so we can flee at the drop of a hat?

An institutional example of hyperreactivity is the Cold War practice of deterrence in which both the United States and the Soviet Union spent forty-five years building up ever more monstrous caches of nuclear weapons, enough to destroy the world ten times over, while irrationally depleting their own economies, environments, and the health of their own citizenry. "The Button" to launch World War III so casually installed in the White House basement; the Doomsday Plane to "protect" the President from nuclear war; concrete underground bunkers for members of Congress beneath a high-class resort in Virginia; the storming of a religious-cult compound in Waco, Texas; the counterurge within the compound to amass a cache of high-power weapons; President Clinton's retaliatory attack on Iraq for a crime never committed—all are expressions of the hyperreactivity that is characteristic of post-traumatic stress.

Recurrent intrusive recollections of trauma, flashbacks, and nightmares. These are projections of the effects of past trauma into the present or future. Such symptoms are best known in survivors of war who, years after service, jump behind a bush on Main Street in full combat posture or fall from bed shrieking in terror. As adults, survivors of childhood sexual abuse might burst into tears or collapse in anxiety while making love. Those who endured the Buffalo Creek disaster report nightmares of death and destruction for years after the event. "Since the flood I have dreams, you know," said one person. "I dream I'm running from death, I'm always running from death."[11]

On the collective level, the principle channels of shared memory, vision, and projection are television and film, and these, like the death-dreamer from Buffalo Creek, regularly deliver intrusive images of violence and stress. You and I are perfectly capable of producing images of monsters and war ourselves. At this point in the development of civilization, though, our individual imaginations are not even needed to generate frightening flashbacks.

All we have to do is turn on the TV or go to the movies to feed our psyches with bloody shoot-outs, terrorizing monsters, and an unending pitting of good against evil—otherwise known as tame against wild. *Home Alone. The Hand That Rocks the Cradle. Fatal Attraction. Lethal Weapon.* Cop shows. Monster shows. Law shows. Now there are television programs solely devoted to displaying real-life traumatizing situations and their rescues. Apart from small-scale solitary attempts to change such programming, this outpouring of traumatic themes falls upon accepting psyches; as a society, we assume them as routine and relentlessly spend millions of dollars to consume more of them.

Psychic numbing, constriction of feeling, warding off of such intrusions. Robert Lifton describes the response of the survivors of Hiroshima as psychic numbing: a diminished capacity or inclination to feel; a blocking of feelings, images, or both. "Of course, I didn't regard them as simply pieces of wood," said a noncommissioned officer assigned to clear human bodies from the streets. "They were dead bodies, but if we had been sentimental we couldn't have done the work . . . we had no emotions. . . . I was temporarily without feeling."[12]

A similar "dead to the world" approach to life has become the modus operandi of most people living in mass technological society. How could we be otherwise, given the plethora of threats and dangers? This is the "poor stiff" caught in rush-hour traffic, watching television, glued to his computer screen. This is the crowd of paralyzed people in the elevator. I always remember my college roommate's first summer job. She was a country girl from Massachusetts and went to Cleveland to work as a secretary in a downtown law firm. She returned to college in September with great disillusionment, shaking her head about the comotose people on the bus, in the streets, everywhere in the city. When the Walkman first became popular in the 1980s, I, having seen a few too many Fred Astaire–Ginger Rogers films, imagined everyone dancing down the aisles of supermarkets, across freeway meridians, in the halls of corporations; instead, solitary audio entertainment seemed only to add to our emotional deadness and isolation.

On an institutional level, we have the military commander coldly calculating strategies that endanger thousands, perhaps millions, of lives. We have corporate executives plotting the demise of whole ecosysytems with graphs and charts. We have government representatives listening like wooden robots to citizens' tearful pleas about technological disaster after technological disaster. Psychiatrists Lifton and Jerome Frank describe the constriction of feeling that lays the basis for the bizarre capacity to inflict *more* trauma by sending more young men to war and producing more nuclear weapons,[13] and as Stanley Diamond puts it, "Modern mass society creates the modern mass soldier."[14]

A sense of powerlessness over one's destiny, a sense of futurelessness, and surrender patterns. These signal the triumph of victimization in the survivor's psyche—the belief, rooted in the reality of the original experience, that nothing can be done to stop the flood, explosion, war, rapist, bombing, attack. . . . As Kai Erikson puts it, "Against all that force and animus, the person has no defense other than to make himself small, to draw a curtain over his sensory organs, to take his inner self out of the field of combat so that there is less of him to be wounded and less of him to be implicated in the insanity of what is happening."[15]

Paradoxically, the prevalence of stories of superhuman heroism in western culture reveals this same theme of powerlessness in our collective psyche. Robin Hood. Superman. Rambo. Despite the inspiration these stories are ostensibly meant to provide, the underlying predicament they unveil is the presence of massively unbeatable odds—and a popular sense of overwhelm and resignation before them.

If we remove the *deus ex machina* of the hero, we witness this same sense of powerlessness in widespread alienation from involvement in social issues, declining participation in the electoral process, a public content to passively witness acts of violence against individuals in the streets and corporate destruction of the Earth. If God died at the turn of the twentieth century, the hero seems to be dying at the turn of the twenty-first, and in his place the up-against-the-wall, deluged-by-unsolvable-problems nature of our situation is revealed. We find a growing sense, confirmed by actual developments, that there is no future in an age of mass society, multinational takeover, military dominance, unrelenting development, and ecological disaster.

Arrested genetic and/or psychosocial development. When a traumatic experience occurs at a critical stage of an individual's development, it tends to truncate completion of that stage, causing the person to limp along into the future without benefit of the particular ability or insight that is normally acquired. As I have already mentioned, the social dislocations associated with domestication broke the continuity of a millennia-old way of raising children, causing disjunction in the built-in synchronicity between the child's expectations for development and cultural supports provided for that development.

It should not surprise us that evidence for arrested development in individuals abounds in today's world. Psychotherapy, with its emphasis on dredging up childhood issues, is *based* on the assumption that developmental stages are incomplete, and we all have become so accustomed to forty- and fifty-year-olds displaying infantile behaviors—withdrawing from relationships for no apparent reason, conducting hurtful affairs, manufacturing familial drama in professional settings—that we are tempted to think of such behavior as untrammeled human nature.

This same genre of truncated behavior characterizes our society and its institutions. The United States is commonly referred to as "childish" and "a teenager" among nations. Acts of petty revenge between governments are no different from a child's "hitting back," and sudden military attacks may appear, to the mature observer, like temper tantrums. Supranational corporations find it impossible to admit wrongdoing when their activities or products damage people and communities. And what lies behind the perverse delight so many corporations seem to take in pummeling, scraping, and assaulting the Earth?

Narcissism. According to Erich Fromm, this is "a state of experience in which only the person himself, *his* body, *his* needs, *his* feelings, *his* thoughts, *his* property, everything and everybody pertaining to *him* are experienced as fully real, while everybody and everything that does not form part of his needs is not interesting, not fully real, is perceived only by intellectual recognition."[16]

As an outgrowth of the traumatic experience, the origins of narcissism are not difficult to locate. The satisfaction of one's needs for security, integrity, and communion is truncated, leaving the individual in such a needy state that she can survive only by "looking out for Number One." The result? A plethora of raving egotists among us—and less obviously, those whose obsessive strivings for recognition are hidden behind social validation, even acclaim. The cult of the celebrity projects needy superstars—just as it titillates a needy public with the possibility of seeing a star in a restaurant. The political system provides a ready springboard for narcissists striving to produce power over their audiences for the sake of salving their own desperation.

The individualism our society touts as the pinnacle of evolutionary achievement is a bold-faced expression of narcissism. Never in the history of humanity has so much emphasis, attention, and responsibility fallen upon the individual; never before has there been so much isolation of the individual. In his critique of American individualism, sociologist Philip Slater lays out three universal urges that are frustrated in today's world: the urge for community, the urge for engagement, and the urge for shared responsibility and interdependence[17]—not surprisingly, the very qualities that have slipped away from grasp in the last ten thousand years of history.

Thinking disorders. The thinking disorders that typically accompany the traumatized mind stem from a constant intrapsychic pressure to maintain vigilance, ward off unbearable flashbacks, numb one's heart, bolster a chronic sense of powerlessness, and forge recognition in the outside world. Against such an onslaught, how *could* one think well?

The traumatized mentality often includes rigid, overly rationalistic, either/or logic and grandiose strategizing. It may also contain basic contradictions or affronts to common sense that may be obvious to a balanced observer but remain invisible to the traumatized thinker. A man I once met spent all his money on fancy cars, expensive dinners, and exotic vacations; went broke; and, with no job prospects in sight, concluded that the best survival strategy would be to build an unneeded second house in his backyard. Often a person will avoid confronting the real issues at hand by positing superficial choices and comparisons. A Native American man I know, whose tribe was nearly decimated in the 1600s, told me he is happy to be alive today because he can use a computer to research the demise of Indian people.

On a social level, the thinking disorders that result from trauma often involve some notion of addressing a current problem with a "fix" that, any thinking person can see, will bring on future problems worse than those that already exist. Here in New Mexico geologists and hydrologists warn that the water supply cannot support a larger population than now lives here—yet our elected officials and chambers of commerce continue to advertise New Mexico as *the* place to move to, while realtors and development corporations rampantly turn desert land into golf courses, industrial parks, and suburban developments. Mobil Corporation's "news" video *Polystyrene Foam and the Environment* urges viewers to think of plastic as the *best* waste to put in landfills, while the corporate-backed recycling promoter Keep America Beautiful defines trash incineration as "recycling." At the 1992 Earth Summit President George Bush proclaimed that expanded technological development and economic growth "will save the Earth."

Here we have what Frances Harwood calls the "agricultural mind"[18]—a mechanistic mentality that requires reality to conform to predetermined strategies, no matter how irrelevant they are to the whole of life, in the same way a farm must conform to the laws of cultivation while barring the unpredictability of the wilds.

The similarities between such a worldview and the traumatized mind are too obvious to overlook, and indeed their origins coincide. As western peoples lost our place in the natural world, we also lost the sense of interconnectedness and the holistic worldview we had previously known. We began to formulate a new perceptual context for ourselves. Taking on this task not out of the elliptical synchronicity of mind, body, soul, and Earth that had informed our process of conceptualization in the past, but rather out of a sense of waning security and growing terror, we projected a world to fit our desperate needs: a world in which humans maintain constant vigilance, ward off intrusive flashbacks, numb ourselves from feeling, feel powerless and victimized, rationalize our lack of maturity, and idealize our narcissism. We created linear perspective, the modern scientific paradigm, and techno-utopia.

7

Techno-Addiction

Trauma is the freeway to addiction.

—TERRY KELLOGG, *Broken Toys,*
Broken Dreams

ADDICTION is yet another possible response to the ongoing
pain and dislocation that accompany unhealed trauma,
and I give it the special focus of this chapter because of its
prevalence in our lives today.

What is addiction? We certainly know what it looks like.
Addiction looks like a man lying on the sidewalk, soaked in his
own vomit, next to a broken bottle of wine. It looks like a young
lawyer sniffing cocaine in a plush hotel room. Addiction looks
like a housewife downing yet another caplet of Valium at her red-
and-white-checked kitchen table. It looks like a businessman
nervously glancing both ways and then diving through the
threshold of the whorehouse. It looks like a politician attending
fourteen meetings in one day, and then three more that night.

Addiction looks like a man who puts his compulsion before his
family, his job, even his own health. It looks like a woman who
unconsciously flips between "I am worthless" and "I am super-
woman." Addiction looks like a person unable to express appropriate feelings. It looks like a perpetrator of abuse who constructs
elaborate excuses for not acknowledging the hurt he has caused.
It looks like a woman who blames everyone and everything else

for her own failures. It looks like a man whose life is completely out of control, driven by an obsession to control his life.

According to Craig Nakken of the Rutgers School of Alcohol Studies, addiction is a progressive process that begins with inner psychological changes, leads to changes in behavior and life-style, and finally ends in total breakdown and sometimes death.[1] Psychotherapist and author Anne Wilson Schaef describes it as a disease "whose assumptions, feelings, behaviors, and lack of spirit lead to a process of nonliving that is progressively death-oriented."[2]

As an outgrowth of trauma, addiction is an attempt to avoid confronting the pain that lies at the heart of the traumatic experience. Its hallmark is an *out-of-control, often aimless, compulsion* to fill the lost sense of belonging, integrity, and communion with substances like alcohol and food, or experiences like falling in love and gambling. The addicted person is trying desperately to satisfy real needs—but since either the external situation or the internal climate does not allow for satisfaction, she turns to secondary sources. As Jungian analyst Jane Hollister Wheelwright puts it, "Promise is characteristic of drought."[3] The promise of romance, of work, fast cars, fast men. Secondary sources actually do produce a hint of satisfaction, although never full satisfaction—and so one becomes obsessed with them.

This dreadful compulsion is shielded from awareness by *denial*: pretending everything is normal, not admitting pain or vulnerability, holding up appearances at all costs. Psychotherapist Terry Kellogg calls addiction "a process of decreasing choice sustained by denial."[4] This is why it is so difficult for an outsider to communicate concern for an addicted person: there's nobody home. I am reminded of a seriously addicted man whose pattern was to drum up interpersonal drama once, at best twice, each week. He was always late. He showed up on the wrong day. He would borrow a friend's car a half hour before that person was to leave for an important commitment, promise to be back in fifteen minutes—and not return for two hours. He seemed to thrive on making people mad at him. When a friend confronted this man about his behavior, pointing out the existence of a pattern and questioning his underlying motivation, he became cold and defensive, insisting each instance was propelled by its own irrefutable circumstances.

A third characteristic of addiction is an *attraction to repeated trauma*. This is called the completion compulsion. In it, according to Abram Kardiner, the traumatized person infuses his reality with the emotional content of the traumatizing event, whether this be terror or seduction, relentlessly reenacting the themes of trauma in order to present himself with the opportunity to claim the longed-for resolution.[5] This is the rapist who gets out of jail and attacks again, the overeater completing a successful diet and then binging. Such activity is a somewhat misguided but nonetheless earnest attempt to satisfy the primary needs lost in trauma. The problem is that it rarely works; since secondary sources can never satisfy primary needs, they do not aid the healing process and may even become objects of obsession. And since the chosen actors in the present merely represent the actors in the original trauma, using them cannot bring about real completion.

Megamachine, Mega-Addiction

Evidence for the compulsion, denial, and reenactment obsession characteristic of personal addiction is not difficult to find in wider society. Just as the other symptoms of post-traumatic stress are visible everywhere around us, so are those of the addictive process. As Morris Berman notes, "Addiction, in one form or another, characterizes every aspect of industrial society. . . . Dependence on alcohol (food, drugs, tobacco . . .) is not formally different from dependence on prestige, career achievement, world influence, wealth, the need to build more ingenious bombs, or the need to exercise control over everything."[6] Vice President Al Gore has said, "I believe that our civilization is, in effect, addicted to the consumption of the Earth itself,"[7] while systems theorist Gregory Bateson analyzes the addictive process, pointing out its consistency with the western dualistic pitting of mind against body, tame against wild.[8]

I call this collective addictive process *techno-addiction*. The word draws attention to the overwhelming incidence of addiction existing within technological civilization, as well as in indigenous populations after they are overrun by civilization. It links the "death-oriented," "nonliving" characteristics of addiction known to permeate the addicted individual's psyche with those same qualities as they exist in the social sphere. The word *techno-addiction* also names the mechanistic paradigm that laid the basis for the Industrial Revolution, but has in effect guided social development since our departure from our nature-based roots some ten thousand years ago.

Lewis Mumford spent a lifetime researching and writing about this paradigm. He calls it the "mechanical order," the "megamachine," the "myth of the machine."[9] "Concealed within this notion," he writes, "was the assumption that human improvement would come about more rapidly, indeed almost automatically, through devoting our energies to the expansion of scientific knowledge and to technological invention; that traditional knowledge and experience, traditional forms and values, acted as a brake upon such expansion and invention; and that since the order embodied by the machine was the highest type of order, no brakes of any kind were desirable. . . . Only the present counted, and continual change was needed in order to prevent the present from becoming passé. . . . Progress was accordingly measured by novelty, constant change, and mechanistic difference, not by continuity and human improvement."[10] French sociologist Jacques Ellul similarly identifies the central principle of contemporary society as "*la technique*": "the totality of methods rationally arrived at and having absolute efficiency." To Ellul, "technique transforms everything it touches into a machine. . . . [It] integrates the machine into society. It constructs the kind of world the machine needs. . . . It clarifies, arranges, and rationalizes . . . it is efficient and brings efficiency to everything."[11]

A society arranged according to such principles is in sync neither with the primal matrix nor with the Earth. In such a society people have historically become obsessed with anything that helps them to cope with the trauma of it all. Drugs. Drama. Power. Material possessions. There is even obsession with the artifacts that make this "process of nonliving" possible. Addiction to technologies is a fertile, as yet unrecognized focus for the recovery movement. As Mumford writes, "Behold the ultimate religion of our seemingly rational age—The Myth of the Machine! Bigger and bigger, more and more, farther and farther, faster and faster."[12] Fax machines. Fax machines with built-in answering machines. Fax machines that interface with computer networks. Cellular phones. VCRs. Cappuccino makers. Old cars. New cars. New colors for the bodies of old cars. Electronic date books. Jet planes. Nuclear power plants. Shopping malls. Fiber optics. Space shuttles. Chemical weapons. Nanotechnology. Biotechnology. Cyberspace. The technological fix, always the technological fix.

And there is denial. In the face of ongoing, ever-worsening social, economic, and ecological disaster, the prevalence of defensiveness about our society's obsessions stands as stark evidence of denial. As I have mentioned, my last book, *When Technology Wounds*, is based on a psychological study of technology survivors:[13] people who became medically ill as a result of exposure to some health-threatening technology. For my research I interviewed Love Canal residents, atomic veterans, asbestos workers, electronics-plant workers, Dalkon Shield survivors, the pesticide-exposed, sufferers of cancer, environmental illness, and chronic fatigue immune dysfunction, Nevada Test Site down-winders, and many other people whose lives have been marred by technological development.

By all accounts, this population is on a precipitous rise. Two hundred fifty million Americans are exposed to 2.6 billion pounds of toxic pesticides applied each year to public places:[14] in others words, *every one of us*. Similarly, every one of us is vulnerable to the radioactive fallout ringing the globe from decades of nuclear testing, from Hiroshima and Nagasaki, Chernobyl and Three Mile Island, from the accidents and leaks at Rocky Flats and Savannah River, in the Ural Mountains and the North Sea. Along the industrial corridor between Baton Rouge and New Orleans, forty-one million Louisiana residents are potentially exposed to 3.5 million tons of petrochemical landfill and 400 million pounds of toxics that are released into the atmosphere each year.[15] Forty million residents of the Great Lakes region may ingest toxic chemicals in drinking water and fish from the lakes.[16] Thirty million U.S. households—96 million people—live within fifty miles of a nuclear power plant.[17] Another 96 million people have been exposed to the carcinogenic pesticide chlordane in the 30 million homes treated with it.[18] Fifty million U.S. residents are at risk of exposure to pesticide-contaminated drinking water.[19] Fourteen million residents of New York City, Chicago, San Francisco, and Los Angeles are exposed to extreme levels of electromagnetic radiation from the nation's most potent microwave sources.[20] Half the country—135 million people—breathes consistently polluted air.[21]

Scientists assert that the growing rupture in the Earth's ozone layer is increasing immunological weakness in the human species, plants, and animals. In 1900, one out of every thirty-three Americans contracted cancer. Today, after a century of the production and dissemination of new chemicals and radioactive materials, the figure is one in three.[22] The current epidemic of immunological diseases like environmental illness, lupus, chronic fatigue, and AIDS is also new to the twentieth century.

My promotional efforts for *When Technology Wounds* focused on two ideas: (1) people everywhere are getting sick from technological exposure; and (2) since this is so, we had best enter into an informed and reasoned conversation about technology. An informed and reasoned conversation about technology was not forthcoming. While President George Bush's personal physician praised the book, enjoining me to "keep beating on this technological drum," the President himself, newly diagnosed with the suspected technology-induced Graves' disease, sent me a prefab thank-you letter. In a debate on National Public Radio with the founder of artificial intelligence, MIT professor Marvin Minsky, I was asked if I had any objections to computers. I expressed concern that deadly chemicals used to manufacture computers—including chlorofluorocarbons, diethylamine, lencast, epichlorohydrin resin, and biosphenol A—are regularly released into the biosphere at manufacturing sites, and I mentioned a thirty-six-year-old worker, Yolanda Lozano, who as a result of chemical exposure at the GTE plant in Albuquerque had died of cancer. Minsky's astounding quip to this concern: "*It doesn't matter.*"

On my book tour, the conversation seemed over before it began. "Get this woman off the air!" shrieked one talk-show listener. "She's the stupidest guest you've ever had!" "I can't do without *my mammogram!*" howled another. "As soon as we take care of this environmental thing," insisted one man, "we've got to colonize Mars. It's *imperative* for our belief in the future." The degree and pervasiveness of denial about our technological predicament are overwhelming.

Finally, there exists in our society a blatant attraction to retraumatization. The wars. The ever more devastating weapons. The holocausts. The coups. The government-backed murders.

The rush to discover new ways to tear asunder the natural world. The ever-escalating mechanization of our lives. The daily obsession with making public spectacles out of every instance of suffering (technological disasters, killings, rapes) with no grasp whatsoever of the overall pattern that fuels these events. The plunge toward extinction.

How to See Techno-Addiction

In his Buddhist retreats, the Vietnamese monk Thich Nhat Hanh proposes a simple exercise for becoming mindful of the intricate web of connections that make up our lives. He holds up a piece of paper and invites his students to see the clouds and rain and sunshine that make that piece of paper what it is. "If you are a poet," he says, "you will see clearly that there is a cloud floating in this sheet of paper. Without a cloud, there will be no rain; without rain, the trees cannot grow; and without trees, we cannot make paper. . . . If we look into this sheet of paper even more deeply, we can see the sunshine in it. If the sunshine is not there, the forest cannot grow."[23]

True enough. In today's world, though, there is more hitched to a piece of paper than clouds, rain, and sun. A piece of paper (let's say this piece of paper you are holding right now) is inextricably linked to the chemical industry: its fibers very likely harbor the deadliest chemical ever produced—dioxin—which may be residing just inches from your nose at this very moment. In the paper-bleaching process, the chlorine used to whiten pulp reacts with the wood to create dioxin, plus some one thousand other chlorinated chemical substances. These contaminants remain in the paper. They are also released into the air and water at the mill site, sometimes as much as fifty tons in a single day. A second possible venue for dioxin contamination is the use of pentachorophenol wood preservatives in the manufacturing process. So when we look at this paper, we do indeed see clouds and rain and sunshine—and we see, residing here between our fingers, the most poisonous chemical substances known to humankind. Our mindfulness opens us to see these same chemicals being dumped into the river by the mill, flowing downstream to the ocean where they join with clouds, rain, and sunshine and ultimately come to reside inside tiny bird eggs that, resting in nests above the rocky shore, will never hatch.

In the destiny of this piece of paper, we see clouds and we see these stillborn eggs. We also witness an unmistakable enmeshment with other industrial efforts. Bulldozers mow down the forests that provide the pulp to be bleached and processed into paper. Trucks haul the wood, steel, and concrete to the site to build the mill. (The lumber, steel, and concrete industries are in this piece of paper.) Earth movers and bulldozers construct the buildings, and then trucks transport the paper to packaging plants, and then to wholesale outlets, and then again to retail outlets for sale to you and me. Trucks, cars, and buses bring the workers to and from their jobs at the mill, and carry them to and from the stores, movie theaters, bars, restaurants, churches, and vacation spots that occupy the rest of their lives. (They are driving to their Alcoholics Anonymous meetings and to their psychotherapy appointments.)

Exercising our capacity to see the multitude of interconnections that lie behind a single piece of paper, we now grasp a link to all the gas stations across the planet (and all the leaking underground storage tanks beneath them), to all the automotive repair shops (and the oil and gas and chlorofluorinated carbons dumped down the drain), to all the rusting junkyards, to the automotive manufacturing factories (one new car is produced every second), and to the plastics and steel and glass industries that are needed for car production. In this piece of paper we see computer and microchip plants. (Yolanda Lozano is dead.) We see the telephone companies with their wires crisscrossing the landscape and

microwave facilities blasting the skies. We see the unfathomable
caches of paper used by these corporations to document their
financial transactions and advertise their wares. (A city is raging
with fires and looting. A man is beating his wife, a child shooting
up heroin.) The Internal Revenue Service is here, with its virtual
mounds of paper. So are the television and print media industries. (The thousands upon thousands of people walking the
streets with no homes, and all those with homes who are reaching for Kleenex in their therapists' offices.)

And we cannot forget the oil that is necessary for all this
mechanical activity and transport, delivered from source to outlet
via pipeline, on ships, by rail and truck. There are clouds and rain
and wind in this piece of paper you are holding, and the oil fields
of Texas, Alaska, Saudi Arabia, Iraq, and Iran. We see armies,
navies, and marines, the Scud and Patriot missiles and nuclear
warheads and biological weapons, poised to defend the oil fields
that are necessary for maintaining the operation of this vast
technological system that creates this piece of paper you are
holding.

What we are glimpsing here is the elliptical interconnectedness
not of an ecologically sustainable, nature-based web of relationships, but of a human-constructed, technology-determined social system whose existence, on every level, is contrary to the
natural way of the primal matrix. "What do cancer, alcoholism,
and the arms race have in common?" asks Gregory Bateson.
"They are runaway systems."[34] And as with any runaway system,
the enmeshment of psychological dependence with physical reality causes irresolvable contradictions and catch-22's.

Technology shapes society in ways it then comes to rely upon.
Automobiles offer us the sense of individual freedom we come to
crave in a sedentary society—and then the entire society reorga-
nizes itself around the automobile, making its use necessary for
the simplest acts of survival. Nuclear weapons solve the problem
of defense in a world of increasingly aggressive nation-states—

and then redefine global politics so that all nations need nuclear weapons for all future defense.

At the same time, society reflects the technological ethos, preparing us to accept our fate within its confines just as it wipes out all understanding of other possibilities. "We live in the logical denouement of the Machine Age," offers Ashley Montagu. "Not only are things increasingly produced by machine, but human beings, who are also turned out to be as machinelike as we can make them, see little wrong in dealing with others in a similarly mechanical manner."[25] In 1894, pediatrician Emmett Holt's *The Care and Feeding of Children* deconstructed whatever nurturing practices were still passed down from mother to child, prescribing such "scientific" acts as leaving the baby alone when he cries and bottle-feeding by clockwork.[26] School has us sitting in stiff rows memorizing information categorized into rigid departments purported to be unrelated to one another. We are disciplined to abide by rules that squelch all spontaneity, require us to control our emotional and biological needs, and quantify our worth with tests and grades. When we become adults, acts as simple and "normal" as standing in line, obeying traffic signals, paying taxes, and registering for the draft all constitute ways we are required to participate in this grand machine.

Perhaps most insidiously of all, techno-addiction is a way of being, a way of seeing the world, a way of asking certain questions and not others, a way of feeling certain emotions and not others, a way of experiencing that is linear, mechanistic, exclusionary, and distorted.

I will never forget my visit to the Santa Fe Institute. This group of scientists left the citadel of Los Alamos National Laboratory with the good intention of applying computer models to such environmental problems as pesticide contamination, deforestation, global warming, and ozone depletion. My host, the enfant terrible of complexity theory, gave me a tour of the working area. This consisted of room after room into which metal desks, metal

Tori Amos- "Give Me Life Give Me Pain,
Give Me Myself Again"

SM

chairs, and computers had been literally hurled, with no sense of how it might feel for a living being to spend time in such a space. The only other thing in each room was a metal wastebasket. I saw not one painting on a wall, not one plant on a desk, not one rug on a linoleum floor, not a natural scent or a splash of color to remind the scientists of the Earth they were working so hard to save. At the end of the narrow hallway, I commented that the rooms were rather cold and gray, and my host stood, mouth open, staring straight through me, with no comprehension whatsoever of the meaning of the observation.

At this point in history, technology, society, and our perceptions are so completely interwoven as to be indistinguishable from one another. Susan Griffin describes this interrelationship by pointing out the impossibility of determining which causes which. "That's like saying my hand causes my fingers," she says.[27] "Technological change," writes political scientist Langdon Winner, "is now widely recognized as political insofar as its effects are ubiquitous, touch everyone in society, and can, therefore, be understood as 'public' in a distinctly modern sense."[28] Dutch social critics Michiel Schwarz and Rein Jansma describe the immersion of society, technology, and worldview: "Technology has become our environment as well as our ideology," they write. "We no longer use technology, we live it."[29]

Standing Rock Sioux educator Vine Deloria calls this setup the "artificial universe." "Wilderness transformed into city streets, subways, giant buildings, and factories resulted in the complete substitution of the real world for the artificial world of the urban man," he writes. "Surrounded by an artificial universe when the warning signals are not the shape of the sky, the cry of the animals, the changing of seasons, but the flashing of the traffic light and the wail of the ambulance and police car, urban people have no idea what the natural universe is like. . . . Their progress is defined solely in terms of convenience within the artificial technological universe with which they are familiar."[30]

Taking this perspective a step further, Winner argues that the artifacts and methods invented since the technological revolution have developed in size and complexity to the point that, like addicts, we have actually *lost* our ability to see their impact upon us.[31] The technological reality that now threatens to determine every aspect of our lives, infiltrate our very genes and molecules, and encase the entire planet is, like an addiction, completely out of control.

History at Work in the Soul

Beneath all these symptoms of traumatic stress lies trauma's primary effect: *dissociation*. In his work on the post-traumatic stress of individuals, psychiatrist Ivor Browne posits that dissociation works by creating "unexperienced experience,"[32] experience that has not been properly processed and integrated into memory. Just as animals often meet threats of disaster by "playing dead," so traumatized people split their consciousness, removing their suffering from awareness—perhaps "leaving their bodies," perhaps going numb—and thus playing dead in body, mind, and soul.

Dissociation is actually a brilliant way to protect the psyche from threats our nervous systems were simply not built to handle, from changes we were never made to integrate. As Abram Kardiner has written, trauma is "an external influence necessitating an abrupt change in adaptation which the organism fails to meet."[33] The purpose of dissociation is self-preservation: splitting and shutting down to avoid total breakdown. As Browne describes it, "Whenever we are faced with an overwhelming experience that we sense as potentially disintegrating, we have the ability to suspend it and 'freeze' it in an unassimilated, inchoate form and maintain it in that state indefinitely."[34]

On the collective level, this same psychological splitting and freezing accompanies the tame/wild dichotomy. Paul Shepard describes domestication as a kind of fencing of the collective psyche, a fundamental internal restructuring to handle the unprecedented influx of loss and pain. "In the ideology of farming," he writes, "wild things are enemies of the tame; the wild Other is not the context but the opponent of 'my' domain. Impulses, fears, and dreams—the realm of the unconscious—no longer are represented by the community of wild things with which I can work out a meaningful relationship. The unconscious is driven deeper and away with the wilderness. . . . The new system defines by exclusion. What had been a complementary entity embracing friendly and dangerous parts in a unified cosmos now takes on the colors of hostility and fragmentation."[35]

As I began to work on my own traumatic stress in psychotherapy, I found that I had split experience and feelings in ways both personal to my own history and also meaningful in terms of our collective predicament. My therapist, an expert in posttraumatic stress disorder, uses a sand tray. She has in her office some five hundred miniature animals, cars, mythic figures, houses, puppets, and trees—and a tray filled with sand upon which her clients place the toys to re-create scenes from their inner worlds. The point is twofold: to bring to consciousness lost experiences and feelings so that we can reclaim them, and to uncover ways we have fenced off our psyches so that we can reopen ourselves to a sense of safety, integrity, and connectedness. One of my therapist's clients describes this process as "a deep-sea dive to a sunken ship to reclaim lost treasure."

A sand tray I created early on in my therapy focused on a split my psyche had created in the face of my father's violence. After looking over all the objects on the shelf, I picked out two female dolls: a dark beaded one, an indigenous wild girl whom I placed inside a clay cave at one end of the tray; and at the far other end, just outside communicating distance from the beaded doll, a tight little blond Barbie, the epitome of American beauty, whom I placed inside a plastic see-through purse. I had been aware of the Barbie doll for years. She was my terrified, brittle, ungrounded, but nonetheless successful self. In her tiny pink dress, she could hardly breathe. The wild child was less familiar. She was the "me" who had been repeatedly raped, who had endured "medical" invasions, the raw feeling, the mucus and blood, the tears, the knowing that had been driven deeper and away with the wilderness.

These two internal figures had not spoken with one another for forty years. The distance between them was the dissociation between two aspects of myself that at age four, tortured and threatened by a very sick man, found communication or even recognition impossible. As the Jungian psychologist James Hillman writes, "Our complexes are history at work in the soul."[36] The split in my psyche was metaphoric of a dissociation pervading the domesticated personality that is ultimately responsible for the mental illness causing perpetrators of personal abuse, war, interracial murder, and ecological destruction to behave as they do. This is the fencing of our psyches—the walling off of the controlled, insecure, ego-driven aspects that arose to accommodate the survival needs of a domesticated world from the spontaneous, attuned, feeling parts that are ours no matter how fiercely we deny them or how precisely we mechanize them.

8

We Create Our Own Reality

You create your own reality.

—New Age edict

New Age world in a Old World cage.

—JOHN TRUDELL,
"Somebody's Kid"

O F necessity, every one of us alive today is engaged in the business of adjusting to and surviving within a reality that is irrevocably distinct from that which was laid out over millions of years of evolution. This is a reality that expresses, and reproduces, psychological dissociation; it is a reality that we might call "our own reality" in the sense that it reflects human construction existing apart from the natural world. Where are we going with this dislocated way of being—and all the grief, terror, rage, and addiction it engenders?

At this moment in history, we stand before yet another technological thrust whose expression, rather than providing new horizons of hope, is blindly leading us toward more possibilities for dissociation and, rather than offering reconciliation, is bringing us more possibilities for alienation. As Jerry Mander puts it, "The ultimate direction of technology will become vividly clear to us only after we have popped out of the 'information age'—which does have a kind of benevolent ring—and realize what is at stake in the last two 'wilderness intervention' battlegrounds: space and the genetic structures of living creatures. From there, it's on to the 'postbiological age' of nanotechnology and robotics, whose advocates don't even pretend to care about the natural world."[1]

Just as Mander warns, state-of-the-art technologies like biotechnology, molecular engineering, and virtual reality bring us right to the heart of "the last two 'wilderness intervention' battlegrounds." The unabashed purpose of biotechnology is the control of biological evolution by manipulating the genes of living organisms. Its applications include the creation of yet more medical fixes to repair the damages inflicted by previous fixes; the genetic construction of racially selected human beings; complete domination over organic processes in a new form of laboratory-confined agriculture; and the creation of bacterial/viral weapons that can defeat antibiotics, vaccines, and natural resistance while attacking racially specific populations.

Molecular engineering, or nanotechnology, consists of machines so small they cannot be seen with the naked eye, with moving parts no larger than a few atoms across. The idea is to direct these tiny machines *into* an organism (a tree, a dog) or a thing (a weapons silo, a nuclear containment building) to manipulate its molecular structure. One of the primary researchers of these minuscule machines, Eric Drexler of Stanford University, touts nanotechnology as the most effective way to deconstruct environmental disasters, transforming them from masses of toxic materials into harmless piles of nontoxic molecules. He speaks as well of nanoscopic electronic "seeds" that will be planted on distant planets, moons, and asteroids and, upon command, will use available elements to assemble space colonies. "In this last technological revolution," he typically proclaims, "we must guide the technology or die."[2]

Drexler himself validated my worst fear about nanotechnology at a 1991 conference for corporate entrepreneurs, a fear that lies at the base of his reference to the effort as "this *last* technological revolution." After reading several articles about nanotechnology, I awoke one night at 3:00 AM with the stark and unsettling realization, as if occurring on the molecular level of my consciousness, of the possibility of using nanomachines to enter into a person's body and deconstruct it into an unrecognizable scattering of dust. At the conference, when asked his worst fear about molecular engineering, with no hesitation Drexler answered, "There might be a war. . . ."

Another new technology in our midst is virtual reality, the electronically predetermined mind trip of the twenty-first century. This technology unabashedly reflects the dissociated process of trauma, providing a surefire perceptual escape into a technology-determined fantasy world at the very moment *this* world needs our full attention. For all the fun and excitement virtual reality purports to offer, its invention is a glaring symptom of the traumatized personality seeking to disconnect, once again, from the pain of this world and to provide an instant push-button means to feed that dissociation.

Another ubiquitous development is the expansion of the "artificial universe" to the point that—if corporations, government, and the military get their way—nothing will remain except super-shopping-mall environments and biospheres-under-glass surrounded by ecological wastelands razed by mining, deforestation, chemical agriculture, urban decay, radioactive contamination, and toxic waste. Some hopefuls call this prospect "human evolution." I see it as the culmination of the ever-expanding human-constructed environment that began when that first fence pitted the tame against the wild and set into motion social, economic, and psychological changes that are, very quickly now, coming to this end stage.

Mander describes a pilgrimage he took while researching his book *In the Absence of the Sacred*,[3] a kind of anthropological field trip into what filmmaker Godfrey Reggio calls the "posthuman age."[4] Mander visited two of the most explicit examples of the artificial universe: the West Edmonton Mall, the largest commercial shopping center in the world, in Edmonton, Canada; and EPCOT Center in Orlando, Florida, the Experimental Prototype Community of Tomorrow, set on Disney World's twenty-seven thousand acres of artificial lakes, artificial beaches, amusement parks, hotels, educational pavilions, and high-tech showcases. The goals of these two "universes" are perhaps best explained in the literature of one display at EPCOT Center: to "help people who are unsure about these changes, or feel intimidated by futuristic [environments and] seemingly complex systems, the . . . exhibits are aimed at making us feel comfortable with computers and other implements of high technology."

The Edmonton Mall offers artificial versions of "the best and most exciting natural wonders of the earth": a water park with computer-controlled "surf," "waterfalls," and water slides in a domed arena the size of five football fields; re-creations of historic New Orleans, Parisian neighborhoods, and Arabian hotel rooms; an indoor jogging track; a replica of Christopher Columbus's ship the *Santa Maria*; and 889 stores in what Mander calls "an otherworldly container of artificial reality planted in an alien landscape."[5] EPCOT is an educational center packed with displays about futuristic living, most of which are designed by the very corporations that are planning to bring us futuristic living—for instance, Exxon, General Electric, and Kraft Foods. Whereas the Edmonton Mall is an unconscious expression of current technological trends, EPCOT's very conscious and intended purpose is to prepare visitors to accept the next phase of technological development. It features space shuttles to tomorrow, high-tech space colonies built by nanotechnology, and indoor laboratory-confined agriculture—all meticulously manicured by attendants wearing *Star Trek*–like costumes and dramatized by booming *Star Wars*–type music.

Brave New Postmodern World

As I read Mander's report of these places, I could see how certain
wings of the deconstructive postmodern ideology articulated in
academia, the media, and the New Age movement[6] do not just
reflect the experience of living in a technology-encased planet;
they have the effect of preparing people to accept an even more
technologized world—one in which life forms may be manipu-
lated to reflect a corporate vision of "perfection"; in which
anything, organic or inorganic, may be instantaneously disintegrated by invisible machines; in which people will be able to
mentally remove themselves from the trauma of everyday life
with predetermined techno-visions; in which the Earth will be
entirely tamed and human-created.

The roots of the confusing, seemingly boundariless world
civilization now emerging lie not in the Industrial Revolution or
the era of colonialism, as some commentators have suggested, but
in the domestication process that originally catalyzed both of
these processes. As domestication turned expansionism into an
accepted, even touted institution of the western world, and
subsequent technological development made global travel, trade,
and communication the everyday experience rather than the
rarity, the concept of cultural relativity as mindful respect for the
miraculous array of human differences fell by the wayside. In our
lives today, the accepted truths of conflicting ways of life are
constantly rubbing up against each other: we watch Yanomami
protesting mining in Brazil on our Japanese television screens
while doing yoga in our Guatemalan peasant pants. An Indian
man I know lives with three generations of his extended family
on his nation's land, speaks his native tongue, practices traditional
ceremonies in a traditionally built mud hogan—*and* listens to the
Bob Dylan bootleg tapes, flies Tibetan prayer flags, and drives a
hot black car with black-tinted windows. During the Earth

Summit one particular Associated Press photo ringed the globe: an Amazon Kayapo Indian, dressed in jungle garb, drinking a Coca-Cola.

Because of unrelenting cross-cultural exposure made de rigueur by technological expansion, cultures themselves have become subject to the fragmenting process that is inherent in the technological way of life. The result: no culture is left wholly intact, and each fragment that survives, or is exported halfway around the planet, loses its original value. Out of context, it can be viewed in only the most superficial way, perhaps as a souvenir or a piece of exotica, as a consumer item or a "ritual."

The upshot is the next step beyond the agricultural mind. Here we have the "postmodern mind": a rootless, undigested perception of life whose hallmark is the absolute relativity of all human-made experience—the very opposite of the primal matrix's caring respect for the nature-inspired differences among cultures and the penetrating sense of archetypal patterning that binds them. This new worldview rather purveys a shaky sense of meaninglessness, a bizarre commitment to the notion that all of reality is "human-constructed," and for all the grandstanding about global community and Earth citizenry going on in the mass media, a profound sense of homelessness. After watching *E.T.* on television in his rapidly technologizing hometown, a Balinese boy told an American tourist, a friend of mine, "I feel like E.T. I want to go home."

Granted, the postmodern philosophy emerging out of the technological juggernaut has afforded us unparalleled perceptual tools for deconstructing what most needs deconstruction—mass technological society itself. Educators Yvonne Dion-Buffalo and John Mohawk champion this development, asserting that the postmodern discourse is "positioned in opposition to domination and therefore . . . seek[s] the reversal of conditions of oppression."[7] Such discourse is essential; in fact, this book is part of it. And yet it is the postmodern *world*, not a philosophy springing

from it, that so disorients its inhabitants that they become prone
to relativizing and deeming human-constucted not just the en-
gines of dysfunction, but *everything* in existence.

In his treatise on the postmodern mind-set, *Reality Isn't What
It Used to Be*, political scientist Walter Anderson explores this
disorientation. "[The postmodern experience] fills our lives with
uncertainty and anxiety, renders us vulnerable to tyrants and
cults, shakes religious faith, and divides societies into groups
contending with one another in a strange and unfamiliar kind of
ideological conflict: not merely a conflict *between* beliefs, but
about belief itself."[8] According to Anderson, this breakdown of
both old and more recent belief systems constitutes the first step
in a global process that is leading to the emergence of deeply felt
conflicts about the nature of human truth—conflicts such as the
now well-aired argument about education between old-line supporters of European classical values and supporters of Afrocentric
and other ethnic perspectives, between those favoring more
community and those favoring more individualism, and on and
on. These seemingly unresolvable controversies, Anderson pre-
dicts, will eventually lead to the establishment of a world culture
in which "all belief systems look around and become aware of all
other belief systems, and . . . people everywhere struggle in
unprecedented ways to find out who and what they are."[9]

I'd like to give you a couple of examples of what this deconstructive postmodern mind looks like in everyday life, and in the
telling, I'd like to convey how its appearance is a dangerous and
misguided addition to an already dangerously addicted and unecological world. A few years ago a Santa Fe man attacked his
former girlfriend in the street. Unprovoked, he came at her shouting, "Cunt!," jamming her against a wall, and when she tried to
escape, coming after her in a high-speed car chase. After his rage
was quelled by an injunction from the county sheriff's department, he began to attend New Age workshops where he was told,
and eagerly accepted, that "you create your own reality."

Fortunately, this simplistic and one-dimensional posture is increasingly being revealed not as the new social truth its purveyors would have us believe, but as a shortsighted and reactive urge for control and self-definition against the uncertainties of contemporary life. "Many voices can now be heard declaring that what is out there is only what we *put* out there," writes Anderson. "More precisely, what *I* put out there—just little me, euphorically creating my own universe. We used to call this solipsism; now we call it New Age spirituality."[10]

After taking dozens of workshops, at a financial expense that had to top twenty thousand dollars, the attacker received a request from the woman that he pay the medical bills she had accrued from the unfortunate event. His response, and he fully believed its veracity: "You create your own reality. *You*'re responsible for your reaction to the attack. *I* don't owe you anything."

In another strange encounter in the postmodern world, a young man who recently graduated from a top Ph.D. program identifies himself as a "postmodern anthropologist." This means he believes that every aspect of human life is socially constructed and therefore relative, mutable, and by implication meaningless. Nothing is universal. No shared human needs or ways exist. Any similarities among world cultures are merely random. When a physicist tries to explain to this man that the nuclear industry categorically denies the medical and environmental impacts of radiation, our postmodern anthropologist denies the existence of denial. He eagerly cites instead cultural differences between those inside and outside the industry, thereby denying the medical and environmental impacts of radiation himself. When I try to talk with him about how child rearing in a hunter-gatherer band in Venezuela better answers the long-evolved expectations for human development than child rearing in technological society, he snaps, "Those stages of development don't exist. They've long since been debunked. People are blank slates, we're infinitely pliable." When I tell him about my own process of recovery from

childhood trauma, he disputes that trauma is a complex, biolog-
ically rooted experience and suggests that all anyone has to do to
feel good in today's world is to "change their mind."

Such postmodern thinking reflects both the detachment,
hubris, and fragmentation of the technological mind-set and
the denial, grandiosity, and dissociation of the traumatized
personality—which are, in the end, one and the same. The
overlooked factor underlying this bizarre twist of human consciousness is that while it touts human reality as entirely socially
constructed and therefore infinitely mutable, its very presence as
an ideology relies on something that is not mutable at all. Essential to the existence of deconstructive postmodernism is the
predominance of technological society over all other ways and
cultures. As Theodore Roszak puts it, "We are, in ways that have
been expertly rationalized, pressing forward to create a mono-
cultural world-society in which whatever survives must do so as
an adjunct to urban industrial civilization."[11]

Without the technological developments of the last three
hundred generations, we would most likely still see the world, as
we did for 99 percent of our history as human beings, through
the lens of the soft cultural relativity Larry Emerson describes
when he speaks of traveling from Diné country to the Ute
Nation. This is a relativity that respects variety, grasps the archetypal foundations underlying nature-based cultures, and emphasizes the relatedness of all life. By contrast, our experience in
today's world, and the psychology and philosophy that grow out
of this experience, create an unprecedented kind of cultural
relativity that is extreme, ungrounded, and ironically absolute.
There is no human body that can be harmed, it asserts. No
primal matrix to listen to. No Earth to care about. No interconnectedness among people to tend to. No unfolding of our stories
into the story of the natural world. No anchoring of human
experience in the patterns of universality. No morality.

On a one-to-one scale, we see this approach being used by a

deeply disturbed man to deny responsibility for his violence, and this is painful enough. On a social scale, we can see the potential for its use by sanctioned professionals to convince an increasingly dissociated and disoriented public that creating our own reality with genetic, molecular, techno-visual, and shopping-mall constructions would be equally as satisfying as living in the wilds of a mountain valley.

The Big Questions

In the midst of such developments—from the first acts of domestication some ten thousand years ago to this final enclosure in a postbiological, posthuman, postmodern world—questions arise. These are questions that challenge the current unearthly notion of human nature. What if the way of being we know in mass technologial society is not normal? What if the personal and ecological cycles of addiction and abuse that define our lives are not representative of human nature at all, but rather are symptoms of profound woundings and grave pathologies? What if these painful expressions represent desperate attempts to cope, and even to heal, by a people who find themselves in an extreme and untenable situation?

And what is that extreme and untenable situation? It is, as the Balinese boy so succinctly expressed, *our homelessness*. We want to go home.

PART THREE

Hunting, Gathering, and Healing

The Grandmothers go inside the Longhouse. They tend the fire, and wait.

—BETH BRANT, *Mohawk Trail*

9

The First Step

When I reached the trailhead and started walking through the
harmonious association of huge ponderosa pines, incense cedars,
and white firs with its apparently endless diversity of
wildflowers, shrubs, grasses, songbirds, and insects, I
experienced a novel sense of rightness. Growing up in the
suburbs had been an experience of fragmentation as roads and
buildings dissected the landscape. The thought that this
harmony would continue for dozens of miles without
interruption was like relief from a headache so habitual I hadn't
known I had it.

—DAVID RAINS WALLACE,
"The Forever Forests"

How do we go home?
  The journey is not easy: we are faced with trauma and
the traumatic response at every turn. At the end of the
film *The Last of the Mohicans*, I sat motionless in the darkened
auditorium, harboring an uneasy feeling about those three people standing so nobly over the Hudson Valley—the last Mohican
and the two white settlers. They had seen thousands of people
shattered by cannon shot into scraps of flesh, hundreds more
hacked bloody with tomahawks. They had been running from
danger, bloodshed behind them, bloodshed before them, for the

entire duration of the film. The woman had witnessed her beloved father's complicity in evil and had seen her sister jump off a
cliff; she herself had been terrorized by constant threats of murder. The Indian had seen his entire tribe decimated and his best
friend pushed off a rock promontory. These white people standing over the valley, I thought, this man and this woman—they
are my ancestors, just eight or nine generations behind me. My
life is made of their lives, my blood springs from their blood, my
trauma is rooted in their trauma.

Every trauma that occurs is an individual trauma perpetrated
by individuals and experienced by individuals. Every trauma is a
social trauma with roots in social institutions and implications for
society at large, and every trauma is a historic trauma, fostered by
the past and reverberating into the future. Our society is made up
of vast numbers of traumatized individuals, and our culture has
come into being through a universally traumatizing process. The
outcome—today's technological civilization with its massive
psychopathologies and unending ecological disasters—is a collective reflection of the traumatized personality.

When I sat down at my first psychotherapy session to address
my newly discovered childhood abuse, my therapist leaned toward me and announced, "In my experience, both with my own
history of sexual abuse and with hundreds of patients, I can tell
you that your condition is not 99.99 percent healable. *It is 100
percent healable.*"

Trauma specialists tell us that recovery unfolds in a recogniz-
able progression of stages that move, according to psychiatrist
Judith Herman, "from unpredictable danger to reliable safety,
from dissociated trauma to acknowledged memory, and from
stigmatized isolation to restored social connection."[1] First comes
the deconstruction of the inner structures originally invented for
survival. This consists of releasing the barriers of amnesia, denial,
and dissociation; making a safe place for the healing process; and
allowing for conscious remembrance, both cognitive and emo-

tional, of the traumatic experience. The goal is to uproot the patterns of dysfunction. Next comes the restoration: retrieving lost and never-developed qualities, capabilities, and meaning; reclaiming the potential to become a whole person; reintegrating one's life into the human community.

When I contemplate the immense task of a recovery process that would uproot our collective dysfunctions and bring intimacy, good health, and fluidity with the natural world back into common experience, I draw strength from the potential of the traumatized individual to heal. I am not a person who believes that if every person goes through an isolated process to achieve personal healing, society will magically transform itself into a humane and ecological entity. The interplay between personal, social, political, and ecological is more complex than such a fantasy allows, the history producing this interplay more convoluted, the work ahead more painstaking. Besides, such thinking springs from the zeal for instant completion to which trauma survivors too often fall prey.

Yet I return again and again to this potential for personal recovery. For guidance. For hope. And because the complexities of the process by which a traumatized individual heals may provide essential wisdom for our grasp of the complexities of social change.

Thin Layer of Dust

Since both our psychological and ecological problems arise from an all-pervasive state of mind whose hallmark is amnesia and denial, it makes sense to initiate the mending process by borrowing from an organization that specializes in this first stage of recovery. For over sixty years Alcoholics Anonymous has made it its business to awaken amnesia and break through denial. The First Step of the A.A. Twelve Steps reads: "We admitted we were

powerless over alcohol—that our lives had become unman-
ageable."[2]

You may know about the wrenching struggle to convince a
binging alcoholic to stop drinking: it can't be done. I sat for
several days with a friend as his tentative recovery deteriorated
into a raging drinking bout that lasted for months. As I sat there
holding his hand, mopping up the vomit, flushing the toilet, I
realized that dozens of people had sat in this seat before me.
Dozens of people had held his hand. Dozens of people had wiped
up the floor. Dozens of people had wondered at the relentless
stream of rancor he was now barking at me, and dozens of people
had racked their brains for a glimpse, any glimpse, of what to do
to make him stop drinking. The shadows of all these people
sitting on this same seat I was now occupying cast an unmistakable darkness: utter powerlessness. There was nothing I could say,
nothing I could do. Except to enter wholeheartedly, alongside
him, into that hopelessness. This moment of hopelessness is *the
moment* that Alcoholics Anonymous refers to when it speaks of
being "powerless."

Godfrey Reggio makes the transposition from personal realization to a view of our collective predicament. "We have created
a monster, and we are not aware of it," he says. "I'm not trying to
be wantonly negative, [but] if you're hoping to make the world a
better place and you get into the environmental movement, or
the women's rights movement, or the substance-abuse movement, or the anti-nuclear proliferation movement, or you name
it, you're trying to make this world better. I'm saying that this
world can't be made better. It is intrinsically inhuman. It is the
world of the machine."[3]

At this moment in history, we are called upon to admit that we
are without hope. Like the alcoholic, we have "hit bottom." We
are powerless before the civilization we inhabit, and we are
powerless over the destiny of our lives within this civilization.
This statement does not mean that you and I are powerless as

individuals. Indeed, we each have the power to heal our personal wounds, to band together with our neighbors to protest a specific technological or political encroachment, to attempt to build human-scale community. What we are powerless over is the dysfunctional process that is so tightly clamped over our every personal and political choice. As Anne Wilson Schaef puts it, "[Step One] says that I am powerless over my addiction. That is the definition of addiction. An addiction is something that has us."[4] By admitting that the sum total of social dysfunctions *has* us, we open ourselves to a stark revelation.

The punk subculture that surfaced in the 1970s in urban centers from East Berlin to San Francisco provided one of the most coherent explorations of this revelation. "We face the reality of things and want to slap everyone in the face with it," reported one Chicago punk in 1983. "*We tell the truth*, and that's something that next to nobody wants to face, *obviously*."[5] Comparing their slam dancing and wrist slashing to the meditations and psychedelic journeys of the previous beatnik and hippie generations, another enthusiast asserted: "[Punk] only takes the thin layer of dust off your eyes more violently."[6]

During its heyday as a popular expression, punk specialized in calling attention to the moment of revelation. Activists shed their family-given names and renamed themselves to reflect their experience of the world. Instead of names like Big Bears or Owl-in-the-Tree that indigenous peoples choose to reflect lives lived in the natural world, Jello Biafra, Sid Vicious, and Jennifer Blowdryer arose. Punk musical groups highlighted the violence of the world with songs about Love Canal, Nagasaki, and fascism and names like Living Abortions, Malignant Tumor, Twist and Scream, Savage Republic, and Dead Kennedys. Marie Thiebault, an artist who describes herself as "a traditional landscape painter painting what I see in the landscape," spent the 1980s churning out huge canvases depicting train wrecks, chemical spills, Three Mile Island, and nuclear tests in the South Pacific.

Such expressions are not really that different from what we read in the daily newspapers, which have themselves become a relentless punk performance piece: RADIATION HAZARDS WORSE THAN FEARED, MASS MURDERER LOOSE, DOLPHINS DYING IN MEDITERRANEAN, EX—MISS AMERICA ACCUSES FATHER OF MOLESTING HER, TEEN STABS INFANT SISTER, GREENHOUSE EFFECT TIED TO DISEASE HIKE, MASSIVE EXTINCTIONS PREDICTED.

Stay with this vision. Feel it in your gut. Sid Vicious. Twist and Scream. We are powerless. Don't escape backward into dissociation or denial. Don't leap forward to fantasies of remedies. The message is hardly veiled at this point. "It ain't working," the world is shouting. "Things are not right," people are calling out. "Help!" the whales and oak trees are crying. When we remove the thin layer of dust from our eyes, we see that the way the world is going, there is no hope. We have no power. There is no future. It ain't working.

1 0

Moose Becomes Me

We are all wounded;
we are all healing.

—Chant sung by Newe
(Western Shoshone) Indians,
Russian citizens, and U.S.
environmentalists;
Nevada Test Site, April 1992

ONCE the barriers of amnesia and denial are broken, the process of healing from trauma can begin. As fate would have it, the psychic qualities this process requires and engenders are precisely those of the hunter-gatherer. Do you remember the words used by one of my therapist's clients to describe the healing process? She called it "a deep-sea dive to a sunken ship to reclaim lost treasure." Recovery from trauma requires the same keen-edged concentration that the fisherman brings to catching salmon with his hands. It is like lying in wait for an elk or a squirrel. To recover from trauma can require that we be as attentive as the gatherer digging for sorrel roots. We need to be psychologically open, to attune ourselves to the flow of the world around us and the flow of feelings and images within us. The "treasures" that we seek have long been hidden; to find them we must be alert. And when we do find them, our success at integrating them into our psyches is dependent upon our ability to align our thoughts, feelings, and spirit.

The goal of our collective recovery is the tearing down of fences and the dismantling of the mechanistic ways that characterize the dissociated state. The objective is the reunion of our "tame" conscious selves with our "wild" unconscious knowings; the integration of the unforgettable fact of trauma that has overpowered our consciousness and defined our relationship with the world with our lost sense of belonging, integrity, and communion. It is the creation of a world in which we human beings can place our feet upon the Earth once again, lightly and with dignity, and return to the great web of life.

The recovery that we speak of when we say, "I'm in recovery from western civilization" is both personal and collective, and as I have said, it is far more extensive and complex than the healing process of one individual. In his work on traumatic stress, psychiatrist Ivor Browne broaches the pessimism that the profession tends to hold about successful intervention in cases of chronic post-traumatic stress. Many mental-health professionals view singular trauma as resolvable, whereas chronic cases involving a series of insults over time are more difficult or, some would say, impossible to effect. Browne views the process of healing from complex trauma as essentially the same as from singular trauma; it is simply more prolonged, with each traumatic experience requiring separate attention.[1]

Ultimately the task is to integrate what has been split—within each of us; within our families and between the generations; in our culture; in our way of life, which has discarded or harmed so many people and creatures; and in our collective relationship with the Earth. Indeed, the adage of the recovery movement— "I will be in recovery for the rest of my life"—is accurate, yet the missing link is why this is so.

When I attended my first national conference for mental-health professionals working in the field of recovery, I was impressed by the comprehensiveness of the work going on. In one seminar room, a minister was demolishing fundamentalist religion on the grounds that it is an expression of the addictive mentality. In the next, racism was being questioned. In the lecture hall, a psychiatrist was pulling the last carpet out from under contemporary male and female sex roles, while in classroom after classroom, consumerism, authoritarianism, violence, and sexism were all being deconstructed. The essential traumatic assaults common in our society were indeed being accorded separate attention, but who was weaving all this good work together into an all-embracing picture not just of dysfunctional individuals and families—but of an entire dysfunctional system? As befits the fragmented nature of the traumatized psyche: hardly anyone. I kept approaching the director to comment on the comprehensiveness of the event but he didn't seem to understand what I was saying. Not yet, anyway.

Recovery is a lifelong endeavor for each of us because our whole lives, our entire society, and our history as a people have been shaped by unnatural structures and motivated by distorted urges. The challenge of recovery at this moment can never be reduced to the personal; it is necessarily cultural, historical, and environmental. Indeed, it is a job that will last the lifetime of each of us, plus that of many generations to come.

The point is to embark upon the healing.

Attraction to Wholeness

To heal is to make whole. Despite a bulwark of personal resistances and institutional blocks to healing, there resides within the primal matrix a deep attraction to wholeness. As I have mentioned, nature-based cultures grapple with the presence of trauma in human life. You may recall that Jeannette Armstrong describes the severance of human from the rest of earthly life as a given in Okanagan thought. "Original human beings are the ones who are dream and Earth—and are torn from the land," she explains. "This is part of our philosophy."[2] Perhaps such a philosophy springs from the convergence of the built-in pain and dislocation of the birthing process with the particular quality of human remembrance; perhaps it springs from some objectifying facet of human consciousness.

Whatever the source, the bottom-line dedication of nature-based culture is the restoration of wholeness. The Kalahari !Kung practice all-night healing dances in an unceasing effort to seek balance between community and world. An Anishinabe (Ojibway) prayer reveals this same striving:

> Grandfather,
> Look at our brokenness.
>
> We know that in all creation
> Only the human family
> Has strayed from the Sacred Way.
>
> We know that we are the ones
> Who are divided
> And we are the ones
> Who must come together
> To walk in the Sacred Way.
>
> Grandfather,
> Sacred One,
> Teach us love, compassion, and honor
> That we may heal the earth
> And heal each other.[3]

Likewise, Jung points to a universal striving for wholeness in the circular forms evident throughout human history—painted by Tibetan Buddhists and Diné Indians, danced in dervish monasteries and BaMbuti forest camps, shaping the dreams of psychiatrists and schizophrenics alike. Indeed, Jung's discovery of the mandala provided the basis for an entire psychotherapeutic system that focused not on the inner conflict inherent to human pathology, but on the urge to completion.

Recalling the Blackfoot architect Douglas Cardinal's recognition of the difference between "the separate reality of Native peoples" and "the rest of society," we come to the essential distinction between them. Nature-based cultures tend to the psychic severance implicit in human life by trying to mend it—by living in ecological participation with the natural world and by creating, and re-creating, connectedness among themselves and the world with ceremonies and healing practices. Western civilization addresses the severance by covering it up, shoveling it under, dramatizing it, acting it out, making it worse, and perpetrating it on others.

With an eye to this distinction, suddenly all kinds of historical events, from wars of aggression and ecological rapings to the splitting of the atom, become open for reinterpretation. With our newfound perspective, it becomes possible for us to review the perplexing dialectic that interweaves like a life-or-death struggle throughout western history—with mechanistic forces constantly pitted against life-affirming blossomings. Could these blossomings that will not be quelled be urges to a wholeness that once was not merely a desperate cry from the vortex of a downward-spiraling dialectic but rather the common urge, the common dedication, and the greatest success story of the human experience?

Think of the witches of Thessaly who risked their lives to practice Earth-based healing against the colonization of the Greek state. What authority motivated them? Think of the emergence of agricultural ceremonies, like the Eleusinian mysteries, that—even as social structures, technologies, and philosophies sought to control nature, hierarchize society, and split mind from body—reinforced the human connection to nature. There were the Luddites of early nineteenth-century Europe heroically resisting the assault of capital-intensive factories and the technologies that would cement despotic relations between owner and community. During this same period the enclosure movement in England, breaking up the commons with fences, catalyzed empassioned efforts of protest. What is the energy behind these arisings? Think of William Blake, Shelley, Wordsworth, Walt Whitman. The Romantic poets identified a deep longing for reunion with the natural world just as the Industrial Revolution was altering the face of Europe and North America. Think too of the esoteric healing movement that emerged in the nineteenth century, creating natural treatments like flower essences, homeopathic medicine, spiritual healing, and medical dowsing.

This urge to wholeness is with us still; in the face of runaway psychological dysfunctions and ecological disasters, it is emerging now with perhaps more urgency and effervescence than ever. Many of the social and cultural movements of the twentieth century are expressions of it: Gandhian nonviolence, the workers' movement of the 1930s, the kibbutz, Martin Luther King, Jr., the antiwar effort, hippies and yippies, the women's movement, the human potential movement, back-to-the-land, natural foods, Earth Day, permaculture, bioregionalism, the men's movement, voluntary simplicity. So too is the vast arising of passion for spiritual pursuits: Tibetan Buddhism, drumming circles, wilderness quests. And then there are today's social and psychological uprisings: the call for democracy and environmental justice; the collective breakdown of amnesia and denial about rape, wife battering, childhood abuse, dysfunctional families, alcoholism, political totalitarianism, the Holocaust, Hiroshima; the rising of indigenous identity and self-empowerment.

And perhaps most emblematic of all: the tearing down of the Berlin Wall.

Of course, the technological system co-opts these expressions, forcing them into a seemingly endless dialectic of tame versus wild. Because of this overarching dynamic, their emergence is typically fragmented, and we are left frustrated and cynical in the face of insufficient success. Yet, let us be clear: at heart these efforts express an irrepressibly human desire for a return to a state that can be made known to us by the documentation of history, but that most especially resides in our memory, intuition, and dreams. As anthropologist Stanley Diamond has said, "The longing for a primitive mode of existence is no mere fantasy or sentimental whim, it is consonant with fundamental human needs."[4] The psychological qualities we so painstakingly aim for with our therapy sessions and spiritual practices are the very qualities indigenous people have always assumed. The social attributes we struggle to attain with our social-justice movements are the very ones that defined nature-based cultures for 99 percent of our existence as human beings.

By all accounts, we *want* to recover from western civilization.

Where Is That Beautiful Trail?

A sense of safety is essential for growth and healing to take place. It is the first quality newborn babies attempt to develop. It is the first quality nature-based people attempt to provide for their infants and the quality they attempt to maintain in daily life.

A sense of safety is also the first quality lost in the domestication process. For most members of technological society, its severance from our earliest experience—in the form of drugs, forceps, slapping, isolated basinettes and bedrooms, fluorescent lights, baby formula, and timed feedings—is the first trauma to overwhelm us, and the shock engendered by these assaults and deprivations creates in each of us a loss of a sense of continuity beyond that proposed by the birth process, a breakage of the experience of wholeness.

For the individual in recovery, securing a sense of safety may take months or years depending on the severity, duration, and onset of trauma. The question then naturally arises: how long will it take us, as a society, to find security in a world that is virtually formulated on violence? How can we feel safe while drive-by shootings, dioxin contamination, and arms sales abound? Weariness about the prospect of safety is an understandable response, yet to not seek safe places or nurture safe feelings is to deny the urge of the primal matrix.

Acknowledging that there is a problem, taking that first small step, constitutes a giant leap toward forging a safe place. Here begins the birth of an internal witness who can provide a haven of safety, some would say a part of our psyches that is bigger than the problem and not identified with it. Oddly, this observer-friend is not unfamiliar to the traumatized psyche. From the perspective of modern psychology, the splitting of the psyche, the "lifting out of the body," and the creation of dissociated aspects of the self, even separate personalities, are not entirely distinct from the creation of an internal witness; the contrast between the alienated parts of the traumatized psyche and the witness of the primal matrix is the degree of detachment. Dissociated personalities are so severely detached that they may never communicate or even recognize each other's existence, and the bearer may be totally unaware of the inconsistencies. The inner witness, on the other hand, resides with gentleness in the psyche, is fluid enough with its various parts to act as an internal facilitator. Here is the benevolent overseer, the wise one within.

If we look at this inner witness from the perspective of the spirit world, a parallel situation reveals itself, and I offer this situation as a way to joggle our perception of the encapsulated psyche. According to nature-based people, a general energy or soul resides throughout all of nature, sometimes appearing as identifiable spirit forms that either help or hinder human activity. When a person is dislocated from the harmony of the natural world, friendly spirits may become disgruntled and angry; they may meddle, cause trouble, even enter into a person's body and possess it. Or they may hightail it away, blowing town with no forwarding address—while hostile spirit people, their antennae ever attuned to disjuncture, may then find their way to the scene. For healing to take place, we must aim to attract friendly spirits.

A Diné friend has told me about the importance of both human and spirit witnesses in his recovery from what has been dubbed "the silent holocaust" of the Native American experience: militaristic, often violent acculturation into the dominant society by boarding school. In the early 1950s, when my friend was a child, the federal government routinely wrenched Indian children from their families to place them in residential schools, usually far from home and Indian country. Here my friend, isolated from family and tribe, was regimented with military precision to a painfully foreign way of life, threatened with violent retaliation for speaking his own language, and sexually abused by the school matrons. He also endured the emotional pain of the seeming collaboration with this dislocation by his own parents, who in fact were merely submitting to government policy. After years of confusion and self-destructive behavior, my friend began to heal when he embarked upon a series of sweat-lodge ceremonies, breaking out of isolation into a community made up of his immediate family, the male members of his extended family, the wider Diné community—and the ancestor spirits that revealed themselves to him in trance.

How we encourage friendly spirits to return to us, or inner witnesses to grow in our psyches, relies upon our ceremonies, therapies, and private reflections—and it relies on our seeking witnesses in the everyday world. The recovery field recognizes a community of witnesses as one of the most effective therapeutic aids. In psychotherapy, the therapist acts as the witness. The rap groups that began in 1970 to address the psychological problems of Vietnam veterans suffering from post-traumatic stress were based on mutual witnessing. Also beginning in the 1970s, women met in consciousness-raising groups to discuss a rising sense of discontent—and out of these circles of witnessing came the revelations of rape, wife battering, and child abuse that have since propelled the study of post-traumatic stress to new levels of understanding. Methods developed for Vietnam veterans as well as reported by Chilean psychologists for survivors of political torture utilize an active relationship between survivor/speaker and therapist/witness.[5]

In *We Talk, You Listen*, Vine Deloria proposes a dynamic that not only would help to heal the traumatization of indigenous people colonized into the dominant culture, but also would expand western people's grasp of reality: Indians speaking; members of the dominant culture listening.[6] Given the long-standing urge within western culture to wipe out the indigenous world, such a dynamic takes on archetypal proportion. The World Uranium Hearing that occurred in 1992 in Salzburg, Austria, formalized this dynamic, with indigenous people from all over the world testifying on the impact of nuclear development on their lands, health, and cultures. There were Tibetans, Tahitians, Cree, Namibians, Maori, Australian aborigines, Newe—and their rapt audience for one week consisted of an international Board of Listeners made up of journalists, educators, scientists, and activists whose sole job was to sit and witness.[7]

A crucial quality of this process of safety-making is re-embodiment: to reunite the aspects of ourselves that have been split apart—the beaded dolls who represent the bodily pain of trauma and the desperate Barbies "lifting out of their bodies" to escape the pain. We initiate this process by witnessing the suffering of our innermost selves, thereby reclaiming our own bodies. We continue it as we witness the pain and dislocation of others. The dissociation that breaks our psychological wholeness reverberates as the social alienation we feel from each other; listening to one another, we begin the task of reuniting the body of the human community. Finally, we re-embody ourselves when we reconnect with the body of the Earth.

Ultimately, the Earth and the community of living beings it

sustains offer us our most potent source of safety. Western philosophy teaches us to think of the natural world as a neutral or "dead" background to the foreground of our all-important human activity. Even environmentalists sometimes perceive the Earth as "that thing out there" that has to be saved so human existence can go on. In the nature-based world, the Earth is the source of all sustenance, the beginning and end of all life, the whole of which we are a part. The experience of living in a world dreamt by a sleeping lizard offers an undying sense of ease and connectedness. In such a world there is no need for soul wrenching or existential torment, no urge to construct random meaning in the midst of a "senseless" universe, no isolation or lack of place. Rather, as Calvin Martin has written, in this world "moose becomes me, and I become moose" in an ever-transforming process whose ultimate purpose and satisfaction are, quite naturally, the richness of existence itself.

The sense of rightness revealed here is not conveyed by the abstracted Whole Earth whose technologically produced image has been emblazoned upon our brains from NASA's *Apollo 7*; rather, it is made of the interactions that occur each day between human and chamisa bush, human and jackrabbit, human and wind. Only on the scale of the senses—the "human" scale upon which our ancestors evolved—do we enter into revitalized communion with the Earth; only in embodied intimacy do we begin to see the natural world as our ultimate source of wholeness and, therefore, safety.

I first recognized the natural world as a partner in this pursuit after joining with a citizens' group to approach our senator about a nuclear-waste dump the government was planning for New Mexico. The federal plan envisioned thousands of barrels filled with radioactive waste carted in flimsy metal containers across miles of U.S. highways, through twenty-three states, and then buried in subterranean salt beds that were already caving in and leaking into the aquifer. During this visit we pleaded with our senator to think about the consequences of such a plan. One of our members, a doctor whose sister had died of cancer, broke into tears as he spoke about the relationship between radioactivity and cancer. Our senator, under pressure from corporate, military, and Department of Energy interests, responded to us: "Why should I listen to you? *You're just another citizens' group.*" That afternoon I returned home shaken. I took my cowboy boots off and embarked upon a long barefoot walk up a juniper-crested arroyo in the Tesuque valley. I had previously assumed that *I* was working to save the Earth. In that moment, in a small act of mending the generations-old severance of human-Earth interaction, I begged the birds and stones in this valley for help.

Then there is the whole—bigger yet than any specific interaction or conception of who is helping whom, and far more wondrous. At a meeting between Indian tribal leaders and white environmentalists concerning the radioactive contamination of northern New Mexico by Los Alamos National Laboratory, Herman Agoyo of Ohkay Owingeh (San Juan Pueblo), spoke of this wholeness, quietly but powerfully, reminding us that forces beyond individual choice are at work; we each, in communion with the natural world, have been called as warriors to bring our talents, strengths, and caring to this moment in history.

He is right. Forces greater than our individual selves are at work. Despite all, the coming together of the witnesses we need to heal ourselves and the Earth is at hand. Political activists are working to bring together people abused by the global technological system—children, women, men, indigenous nations, people of color, workers, war veterans, political hostages, technology survivors, victims of child abuse, the poor, the colonized. I look around and find, as if by miracle, two county employees formerly invisible to each other, a Congregational minister and a Lakota Indian, meeting to plot a multicultural recovery conference and then, in the office, praying together. Buddhists, Vietnam veterans, and Native Americans are fasting for peace on the steps of the U.S. Capitol. Japanese survivors of Hiroshima are sharing stories and medical knowledge with Chernobyl relief workers. Bhopal residents are meeting with survivors of other chemical disasters. Speaking. Listening. Forging a safe place.

When we add to this already-vast process of witnessing and co-witnessing the inner ability of each of us to provide witness, along with the participation of natural beings like mountains and eagles, the invisible spirits of the Earth, and the Earth itself—the available power for healing magnifies. Even amid the terrific dangers and devastations of our world, a sense of safety is born. As the wise women of the Traditional Circle of Elders and Youth of the Onondaga Nation remind us, "Mother Earth is where you are; she hasn't gone anywhere."

11

The Whole Story and Nothing but the Story

All suffering is bearable if it is seen as part of a story.

—ISAK DINESEN

There is no story more suitable as a metaphor for our human race at the close of this century than that of the people known as Penan. A nomadic hunter-gatherer society, the Penan have existed peacefully for thousands of years beneath the canopy of the oldest rainforest on the earth. . . . From out of this natural universe, the Penan are now on the run. . . . Their once pristine terrestrial paradise is the locale of the highest rate of commercial deforestation in the world.

—LINDSAY HOLT, "The Penan"

IMAGINE for a moment that you have pulled down the chain-link fence surrounding a toxic dump for the purpose of reuniting this poisoned land with the wild forest that surrounds it. In such a situation the wild and the tame do not immediately flow together in harmony. We could describe the problem by saying that the chemical stew of the dump has "forgotten" how to be natural, while the trees and gophers of the wild are wise to avoid this deadly way of being. If there is to be a reunion, some form of reconstruction beyond removing the fence is necessary. Over time the chemicals will have to be reconstituted, perhaps with the use of microorganisms and plants that alter the patterns of their molecular structure and transform them into organic, or at least neutral, substances. To encourage new life, the grasses and birds of the wild will have to be coaxed, perhaps with applied seedings and feedings, before they will venture into the formerly forbidden territory. In the field of ecology, this process is called Earth restoration.

In the realm of the psyche, a similar challenge exists, and as with environmental restoration, it involves reconstituting formerly alienated realms. To describe this challenge, Freud used the image of putting together a puzzle. Elaborating on the metaphor, Judith Herman writes, "The hard part is to come face-to-face with the horrors on the other side of the barrier and to integrate these experiences into a fully developed life narrative. This slow, painstaking process resembles putting together a difficult picture puzzle. First the outlines are assembled, and then each new piece of information has to be examined from many different angles to see how it fits into the whole."[1]

Whether we are speaking of seeking safety or of reconstituting integrity, the emerging theme is the process of making whole. The task at this point is to assemble the actual details of the traumatic experience, and for this the puzzle metaphor is accurate enough. But the puzzle metaphor misses the dynamism of the experience of restoration. Healing more resembles the fluidity of storytelling than the exactitude of puzzle assemblage. As psychotherapist and author Deena Metzger puts it, "Stories heal us because we become whole through them. . . . We restore those parts of ourselves that have been scattered, hidden, suppressed, denied, distorted, forbidden."[2]

Imagine a group of people sitting around a fire, picking through their collective experiences and gathering up the lost threads of their lives, telling and retelling the stories of how they came to be who they are—each time with a slightly different take on the details or a slightly different grasp of the outcome. The goal is, first, the remembrance of what happened. Only then can we understand the patterns that underlie our psychic reality and are translated, through our actions, into the stories of our lives. Only then can we create a new basis for integrity.

Telling . . .

For me, the storytelling began with the two dolls in the sand tray in my therapist's office: one, the indigenous wild girl crouched inside a clay cave; the other, the tight little Barbie contained within a plastic see-through purse. When I finished constructing this scene and stepped back from the tray, my therapist asked, "What is the story here?" and the story began to unfold. To begin, these two creatures had not spoken with each other in forty years. One was sitting in the shadow of her cave; the other lay on the far side of the tray, encased in a world of plastic. The distance between them made communication impossible.

I set out to acquire two miniature telephones. I scoured the five-and-dimes around Santa Fe's Plaza but found just one tiny Victorian-style telephone. Although I felt tired and silly spending an entire Saturday afternoon hell-bent on buying toy telephones, I *had* to complete the mission; the wild girl and the Barbie had to speak to each other, and at least for now, they had to do it at a "safe" distance. I needed a second telephone. I then drove five miles to the Villa Linda Mall at the outskirts of town, braved the Saturday parking morass, and at long last located a small "cordless" phone that beeped a tune when you picked it up. I brought the telephones to my next therapy session, and communication between my wild and domesticated selves was launched. In the months to follow, an unprecedented ability to do the work of trauma recovery arose. I told the stories of the horrific events of my childhood—the death threats, the calculated rapings, the blood extractions, the surgery my father performed on me for no rational reason. I expressed feelings about these events and accepted their reality, and I learned how my repressed "wild" self and my conscious "tame" self had managed miraculously to survive.

The memories come like ghostly threads, each a smoky wisp snaking its way back into consciousness as a flashback, a dream, a feeling, a hunch. They come slowly and in pieces for the very reason that the trauma experience shatters into fragments in the first place: the pain of knowing is too overwhelming to bear and, in some cases, the threat of retribution too great.

Occasionally a breakthrough takes place when several threads suddenly intertwine to reveal a previously unknown story. This happened quite spectacularly for a client of mine who had been working on the psychic effects of her mother's volatile rage. Every now and again she would stop and ponder, "There's something else, I know there is—but I don't know what it is," and then retreat from exploring what this something else might be. One afternoon she closed her eyes and saw in her mind's eye the distinct outlines of a vacuum cleaner. "Something's been sucked up," she explained, "and now it's gone." I reminded her that vacuum cleaners have a zipper, and as unpleasant as such a task might seem, unzipping the outer bag, removing the inner bag, and breaking it open to reveal the contents *was* an option. She didn't want to pursue it, and for the next year we focused on piecing together the family events we already knew about.

Then one day my client arrived at the office and again stated that she did not yet have the whole story. Sensing something different in her, I looked her in the eye and asked, "What happened? Where? When?" She looked searingly back at me and stated, "My father's friend raped me. It happened at Coney Island under the Boardwalk when I was seven. It happened more than once."

The process of discovering these long-lost stories reawakens in us a trust in the flow and timing of the primal matrix. Our stories do not typically come to consciousness in fast-forward, for once the psyche begins to heal, it is constantly shifting its attention between releasing the stories from repression, receiving them into consciousness, and building strength for their acceptance. Once healing begins, though, each memory that bubbles up no longer explodes like an emotional bombshell; it is now part of a flow of vitality—with each new revelation relating to the ones that have come before, to those following, and to those arriving at the same time.

The task of re-embodiment, begun as an essential facet of the safety-making process, accompanies this unfolding of memory. I was not surprised at the timing my psyche chose to present me with the actual physical pain of my father's rapings and "medical" invasions. A week before I had come to a crucial insight: the difference between everyday reverie and splitting into a dissociated state. One night as I lay in bed, I noticed myself "lifting out of my body." Because of the healing work I was doing, I immediately recognized that I was not nodding off into blissful reverie; *I was dissociating*. The catalyst for dissociation was fear: a feeling that was being catalyzed by current events in my life, but that was so painfully reminiscent of the terror I experienced under my father's authority that I immediately fled "up" and "out." A realization of seemingly subtle proportion but a turning point nonetheless, and I was able to guide my consciousness back to my body to embrace the fear. My psyche kindly waited a week—and then it delivered to me the full-bodied experience of the original source of my dissociation: the pelvic agony that had occurred some forty years earlier erupted into consciousness, my body writhing on the floor, my mind opening to the full truth.

As the stories come to be known, the task of examining their content and determining the truth also emerges. This is not always easy. The stories are often enmeshed with attitudes that have been shaped by false perceptions; for instance, rationalizations of one's violence or the perpetuation of a sense of victimization. A man repeatedly beaten, for example, may feel his job in life is to beat up other people; a child who has been raped may feel he is at fault. Such perceptions sometimes arise out of the traumatic experience itself ("I must be a bad person if this is happening to me") and sometimes have been instilled by perpetrators seeking to avoid apprehension ("You brought this on yourself!"). The task is to peel away the attitudinal overlay and uncover the truth of the situation. For some people, this means the truth of painful things done to them and how they are not to blame. For others, it means the truth of painful things done to them, how they are not to blame—*and* the truth of what suffering they have consequently perpetrated and what responsibility they must take to restore justice. The inability to admit to this last truth may be the basis of the current, oddly defensive, backlash against revelations of childhood abuse.

Another phenomenon often accompanying the work of recovery is the mirroring of inner and outer worlds. We've seen this interplay in descriptions of Native American cultures: in the movie *Thunderheart*, when the old Lakota medicine man perceives in vision the entire drama that will take place and then acts in support of its unfoldment; and again in *Black Robe*, when the Haudenosaunee chief sees fragments of the circumstances of his death. Why are people in recovery prone to know this reflection of inner and outer? Recall the wholeness of the world and how its cycles and passages are continually flowing through us as "moose becomes me, and I become moose." In a civilization virtually founded on severance from wholeness, we have little opportunity to know this reality—yet as we come into personal healing, we also come into alignment with the wholeness of the world.

At the time I was initiating communication between my dolls in the sand tray, a Cheyenne-Muscogee woman came into my life—sturdy, dark, wild-looking with buckskin medicine bag around her neck. I do not like to think of myself as Barbie Doll–like, but the fact of the matter is that even in dusty jeans and cowboy boots, I am tall, thin, and light. My new friend and I set out to write a play to be performed at a literary banquet. The subject was to be communication between Indian and Euro-American women, with a focus on the thorny issue of apology. We never finished our play, but the creative process had us on the telephone, usually for three hours at a stretch and often into the wee hours, long-distance, Tesuque to Washington, D.C. We discussed the traumas and tragedies of our lives; what it means to be Indian; what it means to be Euro-American; and our interests and activities over the last forty-odd years—the exact subjects the wild beaded girl and the blond Barbie were exploring on an intrapsychic level in therapy.

. . . And Telling . . .

The primal matrix is remarkable in its ability to guide recovery. Despite a prevailing lack of guidance, this same process of tearing down the fences of amnesia, gathering up the lost threads, telling the stories, and separating truth from falsehood has been invented and reinvented by groups of survivors of collective traumas.

The relationship of American Jews to the Holocaust is a case in point. The last message the outside world received from the Warsaw Ghetto read: "The world is silent; the world *knows* (it is inconceivable that it should not) and stays silent; God's vicar in the Vatican is silent, the American Jews are silent. Their silence is incomprehensible and horrifying."[3]

Many Jews in the United States ignored the Holocaust during the war and "forgot" it afterward. With the exception of a photo essay or two in *Life* magazine or an editorial in the *New York Times*, the mainstream media joined this collective "forgetting" and contributed to it. History books did not highlight the Holocaust. (I remember a one-sentence mention and a grainy photograph of barbed-wire fences in a history textbook twenty years after the fact.) On the whole, the Jewish population of the country continued, as before, to focus on its prewar striving for assimilation, eschewing the tasks of questioning and grieving as if they might postpone the longed-for goal. Author Shana Penn, born in 1955, describes the phenomenon this way: "The disconnection has turned my family into awkward Americans," she explains, "incapable of the expectation of success and worried that their future in the new world might be filled with loss as well. I never saw my grandparents grieve. My family carried sorrow and shame which they did not share with each other and could not touch. They turned their backs on the past and ignored the shadows that lingered."[4]

Horrified and disappointed, psychologist and death-camp survivor Bruno Bettelheim identified three psychological mechanisms that gave the silence shape: (1) denial of the potential universal implications of the Holocaust by asserting it was committed by a contained group of perverted individuals; (2) denial of the activities in the death camps by declaring them exaggerated; and (3) outward acceptance of the reality of the Holocaust and inner repression of a full grasp of its horror.[5] A fourth mechanism can now be added to the list: outright denial of the existence of the Holocaust at all.

In the same way that personal memory can resurface after the traumatized psyche has unsuccessfully attempted to reconstitute itself, remembrance of the massive traumatization of the Holocaust resurfaced both within the Jewish community and in popular awareness. For one thing, survivors in both the United States and Europe began to seek witness. For another, children of the Holocaust generation began to ask questions. Like ghostly threads snaking their way back to consciousness, the stories returned in plays, movies, and books. The works of Elie Weisel, Hannah Arendt, and Viktor Frankl contributed to this awakening. George Segal's concentration-camp sculptures catapulted viewers into a stark reckoning. Historians launched efforts to reconstruct the events of the death camps while documents could still be attained and before the last survivors died off. American Jews actively sought to reclaim buried aspects of their identity by traveling to Auschwitz and Dachau.

Deena Metzger made such a pilgrimage in 1989, taking five weeks to visit ten death camps across northern Europe, all along asking the questions that the Holocaust, once sprung from the confines of denial, begs us to ask. What resides within the human heart that is so terrible it dare not be broached? What are the particulars of those psyches capable of enacting such horrors? Why the Jews—and how can Jewish people avoid feeling "at fault"? What is the relationship between the Nazi mind and the technocratic mind that produces gene-splicing technologies and nuclear weapons? What is evil?

"I *had* to go to the camps," she tells me four years after her journey. "Until I was there, *in those places*, I could never have known for sure that it happened and what it was. I wanted to confront the worst that human beings have ever done to each other and the worst that human beings have ever suffered. I wanted something—*redemption* isn't the right word, maybe *direction*—so I could go on."

Within the fences of the camps, craters and indentations in the ground signal the presence of mass burial grounds. During her visit to Majdanek in Poland, Metzger sat for some hours upon a crater that was the grave of 18,400 Jews shot and shoveled into the earth in a single night. As she sat there, the words *never again* sprung to mind. She sensed that this was not the *never again* righteously chanted by Jewish political activists. This *never again* seemed to answer all the questions Metzger had brought on her journey. "Never again must we allow the circumstances to occur which lead to the creation of Nazis; never again can we allow for people to be so injured that they become Nazis."[6]

As befits the assertiveness that arises when survivors piece together the fragments of their shared trauma, American Jews joined with Jews and non-Jews around the world in 1985 to protest President Ronald Reagan's proposed visit to a cemetery of S.S. officers. On the fiftieth anniversary of the Warsaw Ghetto Uprising, the Holocaust Museum opened in Washington, D.C.

In an astonishingly similar process of latency, remembrance, and assimilation, Vietnam veterans invented means for reconstructing and bringing truth to their traumatizing war experiences. After outreach centers initiated the storytelling within the veteran population, public forms for exploring, reconstructing, and making sense of personal and collective history also emerged. Films like *Apocalypse Now* and *Born on the Fourth of July* became major catalysts for this process. A line in Oliver Stone's *Platoon* inspired a California veteran named Fredy Champagne to realize a dream. The star in the movie boards the jet that will take him back to the States, and glancing out the window at the terrible destruction wrought upon the Vietnamese countryside, he mutters, "One day I will return to this place to repair the damage we have inflicted." Champagne became haunted by the prospect of doing just this. In 1989, he launched the first in a series of pilgrimages of U.S. vets returning to Vietnam to build hospitals where deadly conflict had once reigned.

According to David Gallup, a former marine who undertook the journey:

I visited the battlefields I fought on twenty-three years ago. I stood, remarkably, shaking hands and talking with a Viet Cong officer who had opposed me and my fellow Marines during Operation Pipestone Canyon in 1969—on the very ground we fought each other. I visited the memorial at My Lai and paid my respects to not only the 504 Vietnamese who were murdered there, but to all the senseless casualties of that war. I had made many, many friends in Vietnam. But had I changed?

One friend in particular cleared the muddy waters of my dilemma. Ray, a fellow Vietnam combat veteran who suffers from severe post-traumatic stress disorder, had told me, in no uncertain terms, that I had to be "crazy" to want to return to Vietnam. I sent Ray a postcard from Vietnam. I was careful to keep my comments general and without detail in deference to his attitude. A few days after returning home, I called Ray. His first comment was, "I received your postcard and couldn't help reading between the lines. It was easy. You sounded happy, content, at peace. It was like you had finally gone home." He went on to say that, although he thought I was insane to go back, he had changed his mind completely about my return.

A few days ago Ray drove to Columbia from Wichita to visit for a couple of days. He said he had to see if I looked as good as I sounded on the phone. During his stay, Ray mentioned over and over again the change he has seen in me. He commented that he had never seen me so happy, so relaxed, so at peace with myself.

I have to agree with Ray. I do feel "different," better, changed. I feel as though I have found my niche. My life has direction.

I am returning to Vietnam in June to deliver medical supplies and pharmaceuticals to the Friendship Clinic in Vung Tau and to help lay the groundwork for future veterans' projects. Ray is going with me.[7]

After a 1992 trip to Vietnam, Bern Wilder reported, "I found myself at forty-two years of age afraid to talk about the big things that were important to me. Afraid to tell the stories of my life. The trip changed me and helped me to open to others in ways I never thought possible. The experience helped me to see that it is all right to tell the truth."[8]

The Vietnam War Memorial, the black marble "Wall" erected in Washington, D.C., in 1982, provided the ultimate public forum for telling the truth not only about the 1960s and the war—but about every single American soldier who died. Veteran activists Jan Scruggs and Joel Swerdlow describe the poignant opening of the Wall in their book *To Heal a Nation*:

The people and the wall met.

Standing. Sitting in wheelchairs. Stretching up. Leaning over the top. Holding each other. Kneeling. Walking back and forth. Crying. Smiling. Staring. In silence. Talking. Weeping. Hugging. Discovering. Remembering. Promising. . . .

It was a time of decompression. For remembering youth and innocence. For talking and thinking. For telling the story of the guy who walked point instead of you and died. . . . For finding that piece of yourself that had been missing.[9]

Scruggs and Swerdlow tell of an ex-medic who had traveled to Washington for this historic event. Walking down a sidewalk amid the throngs of veterans, a strange man suddenly emerged from the crowd and grabbed him, they explain. The man pressed: "You remember me?

"No," the medic answered.

"Well, I was shot up pretty bad. Take a closer look."

"Sorry, brother. I still don't know you."

"Well, I remember you, man. You saved my ass. Thanks."

In the corner of a bar another ex-medic sat sobbing, pushing away anyone who tried to give solace. "I should have saved more," he cried. "*I should have saved more.*"[10]

The book also tells of a vet who approached the Wall carrying a brown paper bag. He found a name on the slab, took a beer out of the bag, snapped it open, poured some on the ground in front of the name, and drank the rest. He lit a cigarette and smoked it slowly. Then he moved on to another name, and another, and another—until the six-pack was gone.[11]

The Vietnam Memorial is one of the only places in the United States where people feel comfortable crying in public. When it opened, an entire nation found a fire to sit around and, at long last, tell the wrenching tale. Veterans flooded the capital on its opening day, and they still do. In their faded fatigues, leather jackets, baseball caps, cowboy hats, and business suits, each one is an embodied chapter of the story of Vietnam, and their hand-made signs and T-shirts proclaim: "Never Again."

. . . And Telling

As we know, breakthroughs in comprehension take place when several threads suddenly intertwine to reveal a previously un-known story, usually a larger story. At this time—just as each of us is challenged to confront our personal stories of dislocation, just as groups of survivors are seeking to confront their shared traumas and weave them into the collective history—massive psychological dysfunctions and ecological catastrophes are cata-pulting us all toward a new awareness: we want, fiercely, to know *the whole story of our humanity.* This too is part of the process of recovery, this need to see beyond the events of linear history so disparately reported on the nightly news, this urge to compre-hend the underlying patterns of our lives.

That I, a psychologist, feel compelled to expand my compre-hension of the human experience to integrate insights from trauma theory, the sociology of technology, nature, and native cultures is a symptom of this growing need to understand the human story as a whole. That you pick up a book proposing "recovery from western civilization" is another. Lewis Mumford gives us an unbroken view of the human story from the origins of speech to the development of the technological "pentagon of power." (How is it that *in 1915* he writes: "The preservation of life is the most urgent business of the human race"?) Susan Griffin creates a vision of the cycle of abuse and denial as it reverberates in both public war and private life. At the same time, Joseph Campbell's exploration of mythic imagination through history, from the earliest peoples to the postmodern, feeds a growing hunger within us. The women's spirituality movement excavates evidence for times when the suppression of women did not exist. As if by miracle, the historic opportunity provided by the quincentennial paves the way for a heretofore unimaginable renaissance among the native peoples of North America—as well as an equally unexpected craving among the rest of us to come to terms with our own roots, histories, and identities. The effort to know the whole story of human existence is made consummate by a flourishing global environmental movement devoted to reclaiming our relationship to the natural world—via research on the biological impacts of toxic substances, protest against acts of ecocide, wilderness treks, ecological studies, and Earth-restoration projects that literally tear down the chain-link fences dividing human from wild.

What is happening here? We are sitting around the fire once again. We are picking through our shared experiences, gathering up the lost threads of our lives and history, separating truth from falsehood, reality from wishful thinking; telling and retelling the stories of how we came to be who we are. We are talking about tribal life, about the archetypal meaning of men and women, about hunting and herbal medicine. We are speaking too of childhood terrors, of numbing ourselves with dreams of domination, of religious crusades and world wars, of oil-drenched seals and high-tech rescue missions, of rupture from the primal matrix.

One afternoon at the 1992 World Uranium Hearing in Salzburg, Austria, a North American television corporation corrals a Maralinga Tjarutja aborigine named Merwin Day for an interview for international broadcast. It takes an embarrassingly long time for the media workers to prepare for the interview, painstakingly setting up the lighting, camouflaging the miniature microphone in Day's shirt, positioning his bright red headband just right. At last, video cameras rolling, the interviewer puts the question to him: "What's your story? Why did you come halfway around the planet to the World Uranium Hearing?"

Day enunciates each word with dignity and a clipped Australian accent. "The . . . future . . . is . . . broken," he says and unhooks the microphone from his shirt.

All of us, native and nonnative, are talking about fragmentation and pain in order to bring about healing. The story that is now pushing through to consciousness is the story of tearing down the chain-link fences and restoring the wilderness. It is the story of tears and laughter riding the phone lines between Tesuque and Washington, D.C., of U.S. and Vietcong veterans building hospitals where Agent Orange once stung the air, of social uprisings around the world mirroring our innermost dreams. After a dismal era of fracture and agony, we are attempting, through our most personal and most sweeping stories, to restore a sense of wholeness and meaning to the human race.

1 2

Earthgrief

Each moment made the preceding moment a lie, but I could
no longer look into the sun, it had already left black moons in
my eyes.

—JANE HOLLISTER WHEELWRIGHT,
The Ranch Papers

WE are beginning to *feel* the full weight of our predicament. Discomfort, frustration, grief, rage, and fear
arise as we tell the stories of our lives. To allow
ourselves to feel these emotions is to come out from under the
deadening of the freeways and nuclear warheads that encase our
emotional lives—and of the mechanistic worldview that casts us
as heartless robots and the world as a machine. To open our hearts
to the sad history of humanity and the devastated state of the
Earth is the next step in our reclamation of our bodies, the body
of our human community, and the body of the Earth.

In the late 1970s, I joined with a group of colleagues from the
fields of psychology, psychiatry, ecology, and religious studies to
acknowledge our feelings about the state of the world. Three
Mile Island had just happened, and many of us were afraid. Each
of us had some insight about our predicament, some skill or
method to offer, and together we founded a workshop model to
facilitate transforming a psychic state of paralysis and despair into

one of passion and connectedness.[1] I called this work "waking up in the Nuclear Age"; educator-activist Fran Peavey called it "awakening in the Nuclear Age"; writer David Hoffman, "Interhelp." Psychiatrist Harris Peck gave it the rather academic title "Dealing with the Nuclear Threat: Small Groups in Large Meetings," while environmental educator Annie Prutzman named it "earthgrief." Buddhist scholar Joanna Macy called it "despair and empowerment," and this name, above all, stuck.

The idea was that we are all a part of the organism of the Earth, with its vast beauty as well as its gripping pain. In short, the personal is planetary, the planetary personal. When we do not acknowledge this connectedness, we posited, we become lost and paralyzed. If we were to express the wells of emotion so many of us hold about the ecological catastrophes and social injustices in our world, we felt, we would release not just the tears and anger—but streams of caring and creativity. In the workshops we showed movies about nuclear devastation, wept and raged about pesticides and oil spills, and performed ceremonies to reinforce our connection to the spiritual presence of the Earth. We took the work everywhere—from American Psychological Association conventions in Los Angeles to villages in Australia. Macy offered it in the Ukraine to survivors of Chernobyl. As a result, thousands of people acknowledged their feelings about collective issues like nuclear war and ecological destruction; thousands of people became more politically active and spiritually aware.

I always viewed this work as a gift from the primal matrix whose depth of insight far outstripped our conscious grasp of what we were doing. And yet a flaw lay at the core of how we conceived the work: we did not distinguish our feelings about Bosnia or the ozone layer from our feelings about the abuses and deprivations of our own personal histories, thus opening the way for a treacherous tangle of projections and enmeshed emotions. I can see, from the knowledge I now have about my childhood, that a large part of the passion propelling me into this work sprung from an urge to make conscious still-repressed events of my past. "Nuclear disaster?" my psyche coyly mused, licking its metaphoric chops. "Now *that* sounds like what I'm trying to say!"

We have a problem here, and this problem refers us to the central difference between western thinking and that of indigenous people—and may be why they so often fall off chairs and logs laughing at our psychological theories. Nature-based people have no concept of a separate psyche. There is no such thing as the unconscious. There is no projection, no abstracted symbology, no distinction between thought and feeling. If a marriage goes wrong in !Kung society or someone falls ill, the onus for the failing does not fall on the individual; it means that something is amiss between the community and the entire cosmos. The all-night healing dances the !Kung practice do not necessarily have to do with curing individuals, although curing often occurs; they have to do with adjusting and maintaining right relations with the forces of nature.

Interconnectedness successfully defined the human experience for thirty-five thousand generations; we were built for it. From this perspective, it seems natural to weep about injured seals in the same breath as one's injured childhood. Deena Metzger explores this ellipse of dysfunction in an insightful essay called "The Slit"[2] in which the mind of the rapist intertwines with, and becomes, the mind of the Nazi. In it, an eight-year-old Jewish girl remembers her father guiding her naked into the shower. She does not remember the shower. The next thing she can recall is fingering her tiny vagina, now so stinging and raw that she cannot even touch soap to it for salve. Throughout the story Metzger interlaces the imagery of child abuse with that of the Holocaust: the father, the vagina, the shower, the body, soap, loss of memory—until the reflection of one is caught in the mirror of the other so many times that they become one and the same. The psyche that we insist resides privately within each of us is in reality a mirror and an extension of the world around us. Psychological dysfunctions and the ecological crisis are indeed one and the same, just as the young warrior is one and the same with the eagle that flies overhead.

Feeling the pain of the great web of dysfunction offers an instantaneous passage to knowing this interconnectedness. To remain caught by the elliptical power of the emotion, though, is problematic. As we learned from Thich Nhat Hanh's exercise, today's context for our ancient inheritance of interconnectedness—technological society—is entirely unprecedented. The agent of its operation—the traumatized personality—is unprecedented; and the results—relentless abuse, destruction, and injustice—are unprecedented.

How did such a setup come to be? As our livelihood in the western world slowly and imperceptibly became domesticated, our psyches slowly and imperceptibly retooled the functions that had previously served connectedness to the natural world to suit the changing circumstances. Slowly and imperceptibly our psychic capabilities stopped reflecting the ways of the Earth and began to perpetuate the ways of the traumatic experience. Projection and introjection, for instance, were transformed. Formerly life-affirming functions that had linked inner constructs with outer reality to foster a way of being that "doesn't break down into anything," they became mechanisms fomenting all kinds of untenable and tragic situations.

Our task now is to rediscover our Earth-given sense of wholeness. We cannot accomplish this by fusing together rape, the Holocaust, and our emotions. While rape and the Holocaust are indeed linked in political, cultural, psychological, and spiritual ways—and this is the point Metzger is making—we, as initiates into a different way of life, do not want our perceptions and lives to be linked *to* them.

From a perspective of wholeness, it is easy to critique western psychology for its propensity to break reality into distinct fragments. At this historic juncture, though, this seemingly reprehensible capacity may be its greatest gift. Psychology excels at clarifying the precise anatomy of dysfunction by prying it from its moorings—the past from the present, destructive personality fragments from one's self, family members from untoward patterns. To return ourselves to the whole of Creation, we must break from our participation in the pathological ellipsis of techno-addiction. We must disentangle our psyches from the myriad dysfunctions that reside both within and without us.

The most effective way to accomplish this separation is to locate the original source of the negative imprint and to discharge its hold upon us by expressing our feelings. For many of us, the original source is a major traumatic event. Combat in Vietnam. Social chaos. A serious car accident. For others, it is severe assault or neglect experienced in childhood. As I have healed from the violations that laid the basis for my traumatic stress, my need to seek out situations in which to express grief, despair, and anger has diminished, and thankfully I have become more resourceful and creative in my responses to life.

The full task of separating ourselves from inner and outer dysfunction is, however, still more complex. Major and minor childhood trauma aside, every one of us endures the insidious, institutionalized dysfunctions perpetrated in the everyday practices of our society, each of which must be made conscious and addressed.

Running Out of Tears

Many of us have feelings about our experience of birth with its drugs, forceps, glaring lights, and enforced separation of mother from child. When my therapist was fishing for the source of the attack that seemed to have laid the basis for my psychic condition, she asked me to search for an assault in my childhood. Focusing on this task, I discovered wells of grief for having been welcomed into this world—amid steel, needles, and masked beings—with a wollop. This is the earliest assault that prepares us for the parade of subsequent violations, for the forcible entries, gunpoint muggings, and nuclear weapons to come. Such treatment goes against the expectations of the primal matrix; we have feelings about it.

There are feelings too about the caring we never received as children, not because everyone's parents did not care, but because the way of child rearing set up in this culture does not fulfill our needs. Then there is the urge toward exploration, competency, and integrity, which, in a mechanized society with its rows of desks and military order, rarely finds adequate support.

The next layer of feelings is crucial. Here is the pain we harbor about our disjointed place on this Earth. In June 1991, I had the fortune of attending a weekend symposium with a group of Native American activists, philosophers, and writers and a selection of non-natives associated with the ecological think tank the Elmwood Institute. The gathering was called "Native Thinking and Social Transformation." Our goal was to explore how generations-old indigenous ways and the "new paradigm" thinking my colleagues and I were fostering might converge.

Jeannette Armstrong began the introductions that sunny California morning:

> The way we talk about ourselves as Okanagan people is difficult to replicate in English. Our word for human beings is difficult to say without talking about connection to the land. . . .
>
> My mother is a river Indian. She is Kettle Falls which is the main confluence of the Columbia River near Inchelieum. The Kettle River people are in charge of the fisheries in all of the northern parts of the Columbia River system in our territories. My great-grandfather was a salmon chief and caretaker of the river in the north.

My father's people are mountain people. They occupy what's called the northern part of the Okanagan proper around the part of British Columbia that is known as the Okanagan Valley. My father's people were hunters. Their medicine comes from that spirit. . . .

We say "This is my clan" or "This is my people." In this way you know my position, what my place is, what my responsibility for that specific location and geographic area is. That is how I introduce myself.

Then Armstrong gazed around the circle and said,

Now I want to know whom I'm talking to, and I'm not going to say anything of substance until I know who you are. And don't tell me which books you have written, and don't tell me what organizations you belong to. Tell me who you really are.[3]

I cannot express how relieved I was not to be sitting in Danny Moses's seat. He was the first non-native to open his mouth, and what streamed forth, from him and eventually from every person of Euro-American descent, was a torrent of grief and confusion about our place in the world. Danny told us his street address in the Bronx—"1495 Popham Avenue, a piece of New York City"—and spoke about growing up removed from his ancestral lands of Eastern Europe. My voice cracked as I spoke about learning to love the natural world, late in life, when I moved to northern New Mexico. Jackie Doyle broke down as she related having to move away from her beloved Maryland because of a broken marriage. Jerry Mander spoke of the rural area of Yonkers where he grew up. "By the time I was twelve," he told us, "it was gone. The paths I used to walk became the New York Thruway."

Our loss of an intimate relationship with nature is not the only cultural loss we sustain. The social qualities that indigenous communities assume remain elusive as well. The sense of participation in our lives and destinies that is built into nature-based reality—this we do not have. If we come to know dignity as women and men at all, it is hard won. We have little time to relax or be mindful. Our food is spiked with pesticides and additives. We are crowded by overpopulation and urban development.

The cultural avenues for developing into full human beings are lost to us as well. Trust in each other and the world, once a given, has become a rare ingredient of our lives. If we are capable of maintaining personal integrity at all, we tend to fabricate it by erecting psychic boundaries rather than developing true centeredness, and while we may be privy to nonordinary states of consciousness, we do not inherit a cultural tradition that reveals them as avenues to spiritual awakening, psychic revelation, and physical healing.

There are many losses for us to name, many losses for us to grieve.

We feel pain about the way the human community lives today. It hurts that there is an old man lying on the sidewalk at Columbus and Broadway. It shocks us to watch high-tech missiles piercing through the sky, exploding over school yards. It is painful to know that every three minutes an American woman is beaten bloody by her male partner, every five minutes a woman is raped, every five minutes a child is molested.

Removing the dust from our eyes, we become capable of feeling sadness for bony African children who, flies crawling up their noses, are waiting for airlifts that never arrive; for the Chernobyl infants born with brains bulging out of their skulls; for the Rongelapese fetuses contaminated from nuclear testing in the South Pacific, pulsing with life but looking more like jellyfish than human babies. As the Chicano poet Francisco Alarcón writes:

> in the barrios
> La Llorona
> has run out
> of tears[4]

We are fearful too because terrorism is rampant, appalled that governments torture their own citizens. It hurts to see the perpetrators of violence—fathers who rape their babies, corporate executives who deny knowledge of their products' dangers, politicians fabricating attacks on their opponents—crudely defend themselves against their humanity with lies. Above all, it hurts to *be* a perpetrator, using one's life to cause rupture and pain with one's fist, with a gun or a missile, with taxes, with an army or an economic plan.

There are wells of grief too about the state of the natural world. Activist Jai Lakshman describes standing in the withering Black Forest of Germany (one in three trees in Europe is sick), trembling with sorrow as if his own family were being murdered before his eyes.[5] Thousands of sea lions in the North Sea are dying of mysterious AIDS-like viruses. One million species of plants and animals will disappear forever by the turn of the century. It is true: men in lab coats inject caged dogs with plutonium. At the Earth Summit in 1992, the prime minister of Madagascar explained to the world that his once-verdant island nation appears from space "like a barren field bleeding red soil into the ocean."[6]

Our Earth is no longer the Beautiful Trail described in the Diné prayer. The Diné Nation itself is parched by overgrazed fields, cracked open by uranium mines, crisscrossed with high-voltage power lines. The skies are filled with soot from coal-fired generating plants; the water is contaminated from radioactive seepage.

Touching the Earth with Our Pain

Our hearts are twisted with pain about each of these things. Pain is the bottom-line emotional pattern induced by our way of life, but because the pain is so unbearably immense, we tend to repress it. Feeling the pain and knowing its source bring us to a crucial turning point. Freud was convinced that catharsis was necessary for healing to take place. Trauma-recovery specialists refer to this phase of the process as "abreactions." To homeopathic practitioners, it is the "healing crisis," which literally alters the chemistry of our cellular makeup. In the popular parlance, this turning point is seen as a clearing of negative patterns so that life-affirming patterns may arise. As formidible as the task may seem, to feel our pain is to come alive. It is to discharge the dysfunctional orbit of pain that currently defines our lives, to touch once again the elliptical whole of the Earth.

PART FOUR
Re-Arising within Us

Let's dance the dance of feathers, the dance of birds.

—PAULA GUNN ALLEN,
"Kopis'taya"

13

Primal Matrix Re-Arising

All at once the silence and solitude were touched by wild music,
thin as air, the faraway gabbling of geese flying at night.
Presently I caught sight of them as they streamed across the face
of the moon, the high, excited clamor of their voices tingling
through the night, and suddenly I saw, in one of those rare
moments of insight, what it means to be wild and free.

—MARTHA REBEN,
A Sharing of Joy

THERE is a stock story circulating among Native Americans
that has marked Indian storytelling since European people
first stepped onto the North American continent. It is a
story about how genuinely bewildering they find the behavior of
the nonnative newcomers. There are many versions.

One of them goes something like this: native people encounter a Euro-American. Maybe this happens in the Pequot forest in
1636; perhaps in an encampment in Lakota territory in 1840;
maybe in 1985 at a powwow in northern California. The native
people are calm, breathing silently into their bellies. The non-
native person is ashen with excitement. He has something to say.
The natives are with him; they want to hear whatever it is that
could be worth so much fluster and flurry. The nonnative can
barely form words. "This just hit me like a ton of bricks,"
he sputters. "You're not going to believe this! I . . . just . . .

realized . . . ," and then typically comes something considered rather banal within native circles, something like: people are part of the Earth. Or trees have spirits. Or as Chickasaw author Linda Hogan's Catholic priest authoritatively proclaims in her novel *Mean Spirit*, "The snake is our sister. . . . It is wisdom to know this."

As the story goes, in the presence of Indians the flash-and-fire of the non-native's epiphany dissipates like water seeping into sand. As Hogan describes the inevitable fade-out, the priest becomes silent after making his declaration. "They still watched him," she continues, "waiting to hear the important new thing he had to say. But he was so silent after those words that they thought he'd changed his mind about whatever it was he wanted to tell them." Maybe, as in Hogan's version, a child sitting by the fire intervenes into the ensuing vacuum with, "So, what new thing did you learn?"[1] Or maybe the attentive natives simply widen their eyes and shrug. Or mutter, "So what?"

The next two chapters are the "So what?" chapters of this book. When we begin to heal ourselves of the traumas perpetrated through western civilization, lo! something miraculous (read: something entirely ordinary) takes place: the spirit-given resources of the primal matrix return to us.

Most of us have known the elliptical connectedness of the natural world, if only for a moment. Most of us have known times of such centeredness that we would dare to declare ourselves whole, and our consciousness has, upon occasion, cracked open to extraordinary perception. But then, typically, we return to the encased isolation our society proposes as reality, and with our date books and digital clocks in hand, we remain there until the next momentary visitation. These elusive twinklings are comparable to the flashbacks that trauma survivors endure: repressed events shrieking for recognition, unexpected and unannounced. Drawing together the cognitive and emotional fragments dissociated by trauma into a coherent story establishes a pattern of integration in the psyche. This pattern then sets the stage for the seemingly lost resources of the primal matrix to reemerge into conscious experience as well.

Until recently, the field of mental health rarely recognized, or even attempted to explain, such reemergences. Much of psycho-therapeutics has focused on facilitating our adjustment to society as it is. The profession's recognition of the need for healing and its attempt to develop methods to achieve healing are genuine expressions, and yet because they spring from within the conceptual confines of mechanistic social and psychological structures, these attempts have typically been shortsighted and incomplete.

When I was growing up in the 1950s, the psychiatrist who lived across the street had a patient, a former jet pilot, who leaped out of his Ford convertible each week and patted its hood. The entire neighborhood, watching with raised eyebrows from behind closed curtains, desperately wanted this man to "get normal"; his "cure" would be final the day he stopped touching the car. Also in the 1950s, bewildered by the emotional undercurrents created by an alcoholic husband secretly terrorizing his children, my mother followed her intuition to a psychiatrist; he demanded that she forget her problems and "go buy a hat." At the same time, nonordinary states of consciousness were shuttled into the forbidden realms of the occult, while people who found fulfillment in the natural world were often considered "bird-watchers" and "fuddy-duddy conservationists."

The 1960s brought a breakthrough. The concept of adult development, in the words of Rollo May, "portrays the human being not as a collection of static substances or mechanisms or patterns but as emerging and becoming, that is to say existing."[2] This refreshing move eventually opened the way for the inclusion of nonordinary states of consciousness into psychological reality. Its arrival also coincided with an independently conceived awakening to the ecological needs of the planet. As Theodore Roszak points out, though, the new developments within the field of

psychology still resided within the strict confines of social relations, leaving out the realm of where humans live and draw their
sustenance, while the rising concern for the Earth was seen
mainly in terms of human survival, leaving out an understanding
of both the needs of other creatures and the psychological well-
being that connects people to nature.[3]

For me, flashbacks representing the repressed qualities of the
primal matrix did not evolve beyond the status of disjointed
fragments until I made a conscious shift in focus. I was lying on
the couch in my office, a warm July wind blowing in through
the screen door, and I was reading Paul Shepard's treatise on
the tame/wild dichotomy, *Nature and Madness*. Ever since
writing my poem "Everywhere she looks she sees man" at the
age of twelve, I had been consciously questioning the ways of
my society. Suddenly I grasped the situation from a fresh and
rather stark angle: *western civilization had robbed me of the central
experience human beings have shared for 99 percent of our time on this
Earth.*

Shortly thereafter, *Smithsonian* printed a report from the Phoenix Zoo that shed light on my insight.[4] Ruby was an elephant
who used to have a mental-health problem. Having suffered the
vagaries of domestication since birth, she had developed into an
unruly resident. She masturbated incessantly on logs, fences, even
backhoe machinery. She lured ducks and geese into her enclosure
with grain from her food trough and then cruelly stomped them
to death. She charged her keepers. She was, in short, a problem.
Zoo officials blamed Ruby's antisocial behavior on "isolation,
disrupted education, and insensitive keepers." Then an insightful
zoo worker introduced Ruby to painting. The elephant took to
it passionately, her trunk dabbing the canvas with bright acrylic
colors in abstract shapes. After she had produced dozens of
emotionally expressive paintings, the zoo held a show of her
work in a Phoenix art gallery, making over thirty thousand
dollars for its conservation fund. What's more, Ruby discon-

tinued her former disruptions and became a calm, adjusted domesticated animal.

The point of this report appears to be the miraculous recuperative powers of expressive therapy; these are real. But let's consider the story from a different angle; this is also a story about the dis-ease inherent in domestication. Its ultimate implications may have less to do with taking up dance or sketching than with facing the fact that the nature of living beings is essentially wild.

With the insights of Shepard's psychohistory in mind, and of Ruby's zoological predicament, I made a heretical conclusion. If I was to become a human being as the Earth had meant me to be, I thought, I would have to become a gatherer.

Despite All, the Beautiful Trail
Most Especially, the Beautiful Trail

The healing process is a spiral in which the same concerns and issues recycle their way through consciousness again and again— each time, if we have done our work well, at a more integrated level. In this book I present the qualities of trust, integrity, nonordinary states of consciousness—and their sum total, connectedness—as expectations of the primal matrix that are typically met in nature-based cultures. Then I speak of how the domestication process truncates the development of these same qualities. Next I show how these qualities constitute elements of the healing process. Now I speak of them as the special rewards of recovery.

To become a gatherer, I began right where I was. I had certainly accomplished a great deal of personal healing and contributed much of my life to social change—but in terms of my relationship with the natural world, I was nowhere. Zero. *Nada*. I could have signed up for advanced wilderness training; I could have pursued initiation with an indigenous teacher. I did neither. I knew not to jump ahead of myself. I knew that true healing is an unfolding with demands and rhythms of its own, and that if I started at the beginning, I would be laying an authentic foundation that would grow for the rest of my life.

I stepped outside.

The first confrontation the civilized person faces is a clash between the insidiously embedded mechanistic mind-set and the organic mind. On your summer vacation, are you going to halt like clockwork at each campsite and count the days, the calories, and the species of birds in a lined spiral notebook? Or are you going to embrace the natural world with a willingness to be drawn *in*? Social critic Bill McKibben explores this same fork in the road in *The Age of Missing Information*, his revealing comparison of watching all ninety-three channels of a single day's programming on local television with spending twenty-four hours atop an Adirondack mountain climbing trees, watching vultures, and swimming in an icy mountain pond.[5]

My first encounter with this choice was starkly metaphoric. Would I don my spandex and tune in the daily aerobics class on TV—lift, one, two, three, four? Or would I walk from my door through the piñon grove and into the long arroyo snaking its way down the mountains? Each of my alternatives conjured a distinct state of mind—the first well ordered and marked by efficiency and product orientation, the second as open as the expanse of the Rio Grande bioregion. The choice I made on any day reflected which mind I was in touch with. At first I consistently chose the TV program; then it was half and half, a little of each; then I found I actually *preferred* being in the natural world to watching television. Today I walk the land every single day.

As native people might say, completely ordinary things happened to me. After hiking through a mile of juniper I stood one day in an open field, my body quaking to the flapping of wings and squeals of the blackbirds gathering there. When June came, I picked yucca flowers and dandelion greens for dinner. Upon hearing the caws of migrating birds in the August sky, I surprised myself. "They're early this year." My lips formed the words just as I wondered how I knew. "Winter'll come late October." Autumn brought a blossoming progression of yellowness. In September sunflowers bloomed along every roadside in the valley; the moment these faded, the glorious yellow chamisa bush crescendoed into fruition; when it withered, the aspen burst into explosions of yellow. When they dropped their leaves, the sky turned crystal gray, and it snowed. It was late October. In December, the whitened earth was delicately marked, everywhere, by the paw prints of all the creatures whose spring days I had quietly witnessed.

Larry Emerson clarified the meaning of these things. Emerson participated in the "Native Thinking and Social Transformation" symposium at the Elmwood Institute. After two days of discussions, our group presented a public event in an old wooden warehouse just north of the Golden Gate Bridge. The presentation went well. Then during the question-and-answer period, a large woman rose up. What about white people's pagan roots? she demanded. What about Stonehenge? The caves of Laussel? The Goddess? Emerson jumped down from his perch in the bleachers at the back of the small auditorium. "You can learn a lot from studying your European ancestral roots," he called out, his raspy voice echoing inside his throat. "You can learn about ceremony, you can learn to feel good about yourself as a woman, you can explore community. But there's a limitation to this approach. You see, the cultures you are talking about were created by *those* people, back *then*, over *there*." He was pointing east. Following the direction of his finger, we could practically *see* Europe, Scandinavia, Russia, and the Fertile Crescent from our seats. "To create an authentic Earth-based culture, we must communicate with the rocks and trees and birds *here, now*."

Everything I ever felt or knew crystallized in this realization. It was one of those moments: if a group of indigenous people had been peering into my mind, they would have fallen onto the ground in laughter. I decided then and there that despite the fact that I was living thousands of miles from my ancestral lands; despite the fact that my most heartfelt community was strewn from San Francisco to Munich; despite the fact that my place of habitation traditionally belonged to a people different from my own—I would embark upon a perfectly preposterous endeavor. I would not merely learn the ways of gathering; I would relate to this land I called home *as if I were responsible for building the culture that the rocks and trees and birds of this place expected of human beings.*

Coming Home Again

What does it mean to come home? From the standpoint of the wisdom collected over thousands and thousands of human generations, it means making this choice. If we are going to refind psychological and spiritual well-being, rebuild the human community, stop the technological onslaught, and restore the Earth, we will do it by making a conscious decision, just as nature-based people always have, to seek the guidance of the beings of this Earth. As biologist Michael Soulé advises, "To whom do we go for this wisdom on how to draw the detailed maps and how to establish priorities and coordinate tactics? Who knows what is precious and how much time is left? The oracles are the fishes of the river, the fishers of the forest, and articulate toads."[6] Acquiring their guidance is not automatic. It requires that we commune, as fully participating beings, within the totality of the web of life. The capability to do this comes to us as we make ourselves whole with the world again.

Already we are enduring the hilarity of native people; they are chuckling at the naïveté of our relationship to the world. Now their laughter is joined by snickering from the side of the "real-

ists." Again, the charge is naïveté. The world is too complex for
such simplicity, comes the defense. Look at Iraq, Bosnia, the
inner city. We cannot do without cars and pipelines and energy
wars. People today live in cities. Genetic engineering and
nanotechnology are necessary for *survival*. The list of *buts* to
profound psychological and ecological healing is lengthy and
compelling. Yet, confusion and cynicism aside, a civilization built
upon the traumatization of its people and the Earth never worked
and does not work today. With all due respect for legislative
measures, legal action, social programs, and the in-the-moment
opportunities for social change offered by state-of-the-art technologies, a straightforward truth is revealing itself. To make
choices about the future that spring from and reflect the full
potential of our intelligence, we must understand what this intelligence is. Fortunately for us, the primal matrix is natural to us, its
unfoldment not unlike the progression of yellow that blossoms
from the roadside sunflowers through the chamisa to the mountain aspen. Despite all the contradictions and the myriad problems we face, the potential to know Earth wisdom and to live
well upon the Earth lies within every one of us.

The creative intertwining of the very complex, and often
painstaking, personal healing required of us with the reforging of
a collective relationship with the Earth is the story now begging
to be told. Carl Jung, whose conception of the collective unconscious extended into the evolutionary, cultural, and spiritual
realms but not into the natural world, came to the very edge of
this discovery at the end of his life. On the last page of his
memoirs, he wrote: "There is so much that fills me: plants,
animals, clouds, day and night, and the eternal in man. The more
uncertain I have felt about myself, the more there has grown up
in me a feeling of kinship with all things."[7] *The more uncertain I
have felt about myself, the more there has grown up in me a feeling of
kinship with all things!* Roszak advocates the expanse of identification that this statement suggests when he proposes combining

psychological and ecological knowledge into an integrated field
called eco-psychology. Trauma-recovery specialists like Peter Le-
vine and Benjamin Colodzin have taken Vietnam veterans and
sexual-abuse survivors into the wilderness to do recovery work.
Spiritual practices such as Buddhism and goddess religions also
open doors to a renewed relationship with the natural world.
Although these practices trace their roots to nature-based cultures, the forms we have access to today were fashioned largely in
response to the encroaching psychic discontents brought on by
domestication. Their impetus then was to reintroduce the agricultural mind to its primal-matrix origins; the source of their
popularity now is the fact that they do the same for the postmodern mind.

The expansion of psychological practices to include a relationship with the natural world finds a parallel, but opposite, development within indigenous communities. Many native peoples
who still have access to wilderness and to cultural practices that
enhance their relationship with the natural world are finding that
the personal problems resulting from colonization are so severe
that returning to indigenous practices alone is not enough. Combining these practices with focused psychological work seems
required. "To seek harmony within myself," reports Douglas
Cardinal, "I had to deal with the things inside that were destructive to me."[8] Yankton Sioux-Chickasaw therapist Philip Lane
describes the workshops he offers to Native Americans for addressing the abuse perpetrated in residential Indian schools:
"Each workshop is a ceremony. Each ceremony is different.
We're the only ones who can heal ourselves. . . . The process is to
dig into ourselves and get rid of the hurt. At the same time, we're
going to have spiritual activities because just emoting and getting
rid of the pain is not enough. We're recovering our power, and
we have to take that power and connect it to something that's
good for us."[9]

It turns out that, despite all, the primal matrix is doggedly persistent in revealing its age-old ways, expectations, and activities. On the deepest level, what are we really up to when we settle in with our families to watch television? Why do children play in circles? Why is fear of speaking before large impersonal crowds the number-one documented fear in the United States? Why do people love to travel? Go hiking? Why, in a scientific-technological world, does Marvin Minsky still dream?

One September afternoon after a glorious rain, my German friend Meret Liebenstein and I carried our canvas bags into the Sangre de Cristo Mountains. On the way up we sang childhood songs. Once at the top, we sat in a lush meadow and I told her the story of *The Sound of Music.* Then we set out to find what Meret promised would be an entire winter's stash of edible mushrooms. We hiked through the woods, earnestly searching under rocks and at the grassy edges of streams. We found none. The air was beginning to chill when Meret announced, "The grove of trees where I found more mushrooms than I could carry last year is just across this river." Ah-ha! I thought. We'd been looking in the wrong place. As we nimbly hopped across the dry stones peeking up through rushing water, an overwhelming feeling of expectant desire pulsated through my arteries. I was excited almost beyond my ability to contain myself, and this excitement could only be compared with the expectation I had previously known when, standing at the entrance to a department store, I was about to go . . . *shopping.* Could this feeling now pulsating through my body be what my ancestors felt when they came upon some marvelous melon or root—and what I had come to know only at Macy's and The Gap? Could the persistent stampede to the shopping mall each weekend be not just the addictive expression we've already diagnosed, but a return, again and again and again, to another activity the human species longs to engage in? And what about codependence, drug addiction, and the myriad other dysfunctional behaviors whose root motivation could very well reflect authentic nature-based urges?

We found our mushrooms at the grove of trees, luscious king and golden chanterelles, more than we could pack into our bags, and as we hiked down the mountain, I did not feel the guilt and anxiety—for spending too much, for getting too little, for buying the wrong thing—that would have hit me in the department-store parking lot; I felt tired, happy, and completely satisfied.

If we sincerely embark upon this journey to heal and to recover our lost psychic inheritance, experiences come to us. There are the developments that typically accompany psychological recovery from untoward childhoods, abuse, and traumatic events: increased clarity in defining needs and setting limits; more confidence; dreams indicating psychic integration; and most especially, a sense of well-being that, allowing for momentary downfalls and challenges, becomes *chronic*. There are also experiences that seem to spring uniquely from forging a synthesis between psychological healing and a renewed relationship with the natural world.

A sense of personal integrity, for instance. This quality emerged quite unexpectedly for a client of mine shortly after she excavated and expressed the underlying impetus behind her anger. Soon after, something startling occurred. She was walking in the arroyos of Galisteo when, without warning, the force field of her body suddenly jolted into a state of clarity unlike any she had ever known. Something like a star of energy blazed; she reports she could feel its emanations pulsing outward to a very distinct end point, an envelope, about three feet from her body. From within this energy field all issues of "bleeding boundaries" looked absurd. She was herself, most definitely herself.

As is the nature of the primal matrix, when one of its qualities comes into fruition, it encourages the others to blossom at the same time and to flow together into a seamless whole. Just as my client discovered this new clarity of individuality, she also felt relatedness to and compassion for every being she had ever known. The sum total of such psychic components cannot be described, not really; evoked perhaps, but not described.

In a marvelous interview that appeared in the environmental journal *Orion*, Vice President Al Gore reveals his familiarity with this kind of experience. The interviewer asks, "In *Earth in the Balance* you describe a remarkable series of experiences, from seeing effects of Agent Orange to being on an airplane on your way to see Chico Mendes just as he was shot, that have informed you about the real dimensions of the collision you describe between our culture and the world. But there is a piece of the puzzle missing for me. In the writing of the great conservationists like Muir and Leopold, there are accounts of moments of transcendent beauty in nature, glimpses of a kind of holiness, that have motivated them. Have you had such experiences in your life?"

Gore's answer, in totality: "Yes, I have."[10]

Lynda M. Leonard, a nature guide who leads people on solo journeys into the wilderness, makes a stab at description. She tells of a trip she took into the mountains surrounding Crestone, Colorado: "When I settled into the place, I could see the magic, the golden threads that connect the trees and plants. This is the beauty of letting down and letting nature heal: you begin to see from the sacred view. You become the center of the holograph that gets subtler and subtler and subtler. You go beyond the density of this reality. Your senses become so tuned in that you hear the ants moving behind you. You begin to be able to be the deer; you move like a deer, and you open to the brilliance of what life is all about."[11]

Such an extraordinary experience revealed itself to me in an ordinary moment. I had been eating a simple dinner of brown rice and greens on the roof when I felt something occur in my body, something like a door swinging open. Wide open. A golden sun was just setting behind the Jemez Mountains; bursts of orange and pink were shooting like streamers through the fading sky. To my surprise, I was sensing the full-bodied aliveness of every juniper and rock and hawk on the Earth. By the front door to my house I saw, really *saw*, the tall piñon that I ordinarily brushed by; its needles and cones were bursting with presence, its branches and trunk with consciousness. I had never before communicated directly with it, nor with any other wild being. I saw how foolish I had been. My recovery from western civilization was under way.

14

All My Relations

Recovery is based on the empowerment of the survivor and the creation of new connections.

—JUDITH HERMAN,
Trauma and Recovery

every tree
a brother
every hill
a pyramid
a holy spot

—FRANCISCO ALARCÓN,
"In Xochitl in Cuicatl"

COMMUNING with the inhabitants of the natural world is essential if we are going to reclaim our psychological well-being and regain the ecological understanding we need to create a sustainable culture. The urge to converse with the beings of the natural world has existed throughout our history and exists still—despite the degree of alienation separating us from the experience, or even knowing of the existence of the experience. Forty-five percent of all families in the United States own dogs,[1] twenty percent cats.[2] According to the National Gardening Association, seventy-eight percent of the American population engages in some form of indoor or outdoor gardening, spending over $21 billion each year for this engagement. The total territory cultivated as lawn in the United States adds up to an area the size of Indiana.³ If keeping Yorkshire terriers, growing staghorn ferns, and mowing the lawn constitute unconscious compromises of our longing for interspecies communion, what does full-out conscious communication consist of? How do we communicate with the beings of the Earth?

All My Cactuses

Already we have communicated with the natural world thousands of times. Scaring a bird away from the garden is a communication. Taking out a can opener in the presence of a dog is a communication. Driving a car down the road at sixty-five miles per hour is a communication.

But what about *communing*? Have you looked deeply into the eyes of a domesticated animal—or a wild one? Have you had interspecies interactions whose outcome, by current standards, seems unbelievable? What about the time your husky traveled ten miles over unknown territory to find you? Or your cat crawled onto your shoulder when you were crying? According to Lynda Leonard, the ability to commune with creatures in the wild emerges naturally when we reside consciously within the wholeness of life.⁴ The evening I spoke with Leonard about these matters, her white cat Critter, notoriously aloof and secretive, made an exceptional showing of sociability by taking up residence on the couch right between Lynda and me.

Somewhat more dramatically, on a winter-solstice trip to Organ Pipe National Monument in southern Arizona, Leonard befriended an ancient saguaro cactus, an act that helped her grapple with her doubts about human-wild communication. She described these events to Critter and me: "When you're out there, you connect with the souls of these plants, these rocks, these clouds, these mountains that have been there for years and years. You settle into the interrelatedness. In the quiet of the desert, connecting with a plant is very real. I found a saguaro that ended up as my mentor. I approached the cactus explaining, 'I'm not so good at this, but here I am. I trust we can have a relationship.' The saguaro spoke back to me. 'You have doubt,' it said. 'The Great Spirit is here. Be open.' "

I had to interrupt at this point. What do you mean when you say you were *communicating* with a cactus?

"It's simple," Leonard answered. "In the stillness. With desire. With openheartedness. It's not about forcing yourself or 'getting it right' or holding yourself in stiff meditation for time on end. It is just like having a conversation. I'd catch myself: 'I'm talking to a cactus?' . . . 'Yes,' came the answer, 'and the cactus is talking back.' The conversation didn't feel like something I was making up. I kept clearing my mind. Since I was dealing with issues of faith and trust, I put my critical mind aside and tried not to figure out what was happening. Rather, I trusted that it *was* happening."

The immediate effect of a relationship with a natural being is emotional and spiritual; a sense of connectedness arises. The possibilities go beyond this. According to indigenous people, nature-based cultures evolved over generations as the result of direct guidance from the natural world. Initiation ceremonies have to do with bringing young people into adulthood in relationship to the natural world. Other ceremonies generate healing or celebrate annual, monthly, or historic events in relationship to the natural world. We, of course, lack not only the training to participate in such communion or receive such guidance; we lack the entire worldview that sanctions its reality. Leonard's experience at Organ Pipe extended beyond day-to-day conversation with her plant mentor into the all-important realm of culture creation.

One day she found a bee trapped inside the thick plastic bag of her solar shower device. With some difficulty she pried the bag open to liberate the tiny creature, which emerged dazed, disoriented, its wing torn at the edge. She then carried the bee to her cache of honey and let it drink. Leonard spent several hours with the bee while it recovered equilibrium. Finally, as the day waned, the bee flew away.

The next morning, to her amazement, Leonard encountered the very same bee; this time it was trapped in her pack inside a box of crackers. It was stone dead. Sobbing, she cupped the tiny carcass in her hand, took it to the saguaro, and asked, "What do I do now?" The cactus responded first by telling Leonard to perform a ceremony for the bee, then by giving her specific instructions about how to do so. "Go to the west," it told her. "At sunset place the bee at the highest reach you can find and send its soul to the heavens. You will know what to do. Give this bee a farewell that would be fitting for a bee." Leonard walked to the west. There she found a stately ocotillo with one shriveled flower, faded to a dried-up hue of pastel orange, sitting atop the cactus. Just as the sun went down, she raised the deceased bee on this flower to the sky.

The ceremony was befitting not only for a bee whose time on Earth had come to an end, but for a recovering westerner whose time as an alienated creature on Earth was also coming to an end. The gift of communion with the saguaro was not merely a ceremony to be repeated for all the dead bees Leonard might encounter in life; it was the understanding that the most important issues humans face—issues of life and death, of trust, wisdom, sustainability, and healing—can be addressed in direct communion with the beings of the natural world. The gift was the knowledge that this communion is not only possible, but readily available. As Leonard explained that evening, "The natural world has intelligence and a willingness to be there for you. There's not a lot of hoopla surrounding the experience; its magic is its simplicity. And it's not just for gurus or Indians," she said to Critter and me. "This experience is for all of us who take the time to stop the chatter of the mind, to listen, to stay open to the possibility."

All My Ancestors

A possibility beyond that of communicating with plants, animals, rocks, and mountains is communication with the spirits of our ancestors. Every indigenous people on Earth takes strength and direction from its lineage. How technological people relate to this phenomenon has been shaped by our civilization's narrow conception of reality, our yearning for ancestral connection at best taking the form of printed genealogies and two-week vacations in "the old country."

In an interview in the Kalahari Desert with a !Kung healer named Toma Zho, psychologist Richard Katz uncovers the native attitude toward our unprecedented deficiency.[5] The two are sitting together in the midday shade speaking about the all-night healing dances of the !Kung when Katz checks to make sure the tape recorder is still running. Toma Zho then initiates a discussion about this strange machine, pondering in great detail how it works. At one point, he asks, "From the day of your birth, Dick, from the moment of your creation, did your elders and your ancestors tell you about these things? Is this thing, this speech machine, something that was handed down to you by your ancestors?"

Stunned by the complexity of what is about to be revealed, Katz responds haltingly. "Not really," he offers. "This machine is somewhat new."

The notion is difficult for Toma Zho to grasp. He takes a deep breath. "You mean to tell me your ancestors, the greatest of your oldest ancestors, didn't give you that machine? They didn't give it up? It didn't come down to you, the children?" He is getting visibly riled. "Look, if your ancestors didn't know the explanation for this, then there's something really wrong. There's something *really* wrong, if you think about it clearly. Look, we guys have our num [healing power], and this machine is evidently part of your num. If we get a fantastically good thing from our ancestors, we don't say, 'Our ancestors didn't know anything about this.' So how can you say that this isn't something great, given to you from your ancestors?" After Katz bungles several more attempts at explaining, Toma Zho sums up the subject. "This is just ridiculous," he hoots. "This is *just ridiculous* that you say your ancestors didn't have a hand in this!"

The ridiculous predicament of living in a culture that our ancestors had no hand in creating stems, in part, from the psychological pain that lies at the foundation of our way of life. When unhealed trauma resides in the psyche, it may seek survival by directly or metaphorically attempting to communicate the pain; it may also survive by denying and repressing the pain, in this case the pain of the overarching loss of our human roots. On a sociological level, the problem stems from the relentless lunge toward ever-increasing technological development. As political theorists Sheldon Wolin and John Schaar describe, the main feature of technological society is not merely the rapid change wrought by the pace of innovation; it is the destruction of things past, the rendering irrelevant of practices, values, connections, and memory inherited from tradition.[6]

In a night circle in my living room, the more the native participants spoke of their relations with their families and the difficult but do-able task of reconstructing their tribal clan systems, the more the non-natives fell into a vortex of emptiness. "I don't *have* a family!" insisted a physicist. "I never knew my grandparents," moaned a psychotherapist. "I don't even know where my family is *from!*"

My efforts to address this predicament were at first disjointed, with one hand doing its work unbeknownst to the other—a state reflective of my still-unintegrated condition of posttraumatic stress. In fact, I didn't even *know* what I was working toward until all my efforts fell together into a unified realization.

I began the work of reclaiming my lineage in therapy. If my father was so deranged, I wanted to know, did something traumatic happen to him? Scanning the possibilities for his abuse, the family history of alcohol use, and the mental state of other members of the family, I concluded that yes, his actions were most likely reflective of his own experiences. I traced the violence back to the generation preceding his and then, lacking any more direct knowledge, stopped. In poking around the shadows, though, I had unearthed and stood face to face with the soul of the family—with all its secrets and suffering.

Meanwhile, I "independently" decided to honor the 1992 quincentennial by researching my family tree. I launched this endeavor, in part, because of Jeannette Armstrong's introduction at the Elmwood symposium in which she identified herself by her clan's relationship to the Okanagan land; it came, in part, from her challenge to the non-natives in the circle: "Tell me who you really are"; and in part from my deduction that if my ancestors' residence in North America dated back to 1633, they must have participated in the decimation of the native peoples of this continent.

I was right, agonizingly so. My ancestors were not just homesteaders who shot an occasional Indian in the forest; they were commanders of Indian wars. The Reverend Thomas Hooker was a renegade Puritan leader. When he arrived at the Massachusetts Bay Colony, he immediately clashed with church leaders over the issue of democratic representation, favoring direct elections over the more elitist choice of leaders by church officials. As a result of this conflict, he and a band of followers traveled south to Pequot territory in 1636. My ancestor was hailed as "the first American democrat," founding the first "government by the people" in the colony that later came to be known as Connecticut. The family genealogy documents his life and accomplishments with: "He preached on Sundays and fought Indians on weekdays." The Pequot War of 1637 was the first major battle in New England, killing one thousand Indians and sending hundreds more into slavery. My ancestor, along with Captain John Mason, played a leading role in that war.

General "Fightin' Joe" Hooker served in the Second Seminole War from 1835 to 1842. He was a raging alcoholic, outlandishly narcissistic, and in constant conflict with his superior officers. A military colleague described him in 1864 as "red-faced, very, with a lacklustre eye and an uncertainty of gait and carriage that suggested a used-up man." During the Civil War, President Lincoln employed Hooker in several critical battles but finally, because of his emotional instability, sent him and his troops out west. Family legend passes the story along with a twinkle of the eye: the Union Army sent trainloads of women out to Hooker to keep him and his men satisfied. Originally, the women were called "Hooker's girls," and eventually the term shortened to "hookers." One question that was never addressed in these family stories dawned on me during the quincentennial: what was Hooker *doing* out west? Surely Lincoln did not send him there merely to dispose of a "loose cannon." He had to have been useful to the war effort. Upon researching the question, I learned that Hooker's job was the appropriation of valuable minerals for military use, pitting his troops against the indigenous people upon whose land these resources were found—a crucial job but one, apparently, suitable for a loose cannon.

This is thorny stuff. Nature-based people embrace their ancestors because, within the bounds of human foibles, these elders have accomplished the remarkable feat of survival and in the process, have erected a culture made of irreplaceable wisdom. On a spiritual level, nature-based people honor their ancestors to evoke the numinous quality of life's continuity. But my ancestors grew into a civilization founded on, and perpetuating, dysfunction and trauma; they knew nothing else. The humble, the heroes, and the fighters for justice notwithstanding, many of them were so damaged that they accumulated no wisdom or numinosity; rather, they actively engaged in the abuse of their own families, other people, and the Earth; worse, they *believed* the twisted stories their culture invented to rationalize such behavior.

It is this alienation that leads so many of us to make statements like "I don't *have* a family!" and "What can I do? I never *knew* my grandparents." Francisco Alarcón, who is part Spanish and part Aztec, sums up this fracturing of family continuity. "I'm a Mestizo because I'm in turmoil," he explains. "We're not in peace. We see ourselves in the tremendous wound of history. Every time I look at myself, I see rape, I see the violation of my ancestors."[7] The question that arises from such an unprecedented predicament is this: how can we reclaim, and honor, a lineage so fraught with abuse, injustice, and pain?

An answer came to me after a Diné friend stopped by my house. The visit was unexpected; a family obligation had suddenly fallen away and he found himself near Tesuque with time on his hands. It was nine o'clock at night when he arrived. He sat down on the couch and immediately launched into a lengthy description of the Blessing Way. According to legend, Blessing Way is the ceremonial held by the Holy People when they created humanity. Placing its participants in alignment with Creation and so insuring health and well-being, it remains the cornerstone of the Diné ceremonial system.

My friend began to sing. He stood up to show me the dance. One song, he explained, contained a special word that, in the Diné language, evokes the linkage of "I" to "all of Creation." He told me how he used this song to help recovering alcoholics regain self-esteem. Then he bellowed out the song, and I sat in my rocking chair trying, as best I could, to receive its vibration in every cell of my body. When he stopped, he looked around with an innocent newness, as if he had just arrived, and he said, "I don't know why I did that." We spent the rest of the evening talking about other things.

Four nights later, just at dawn, something happened. A special moment occurs each time we awake, a moment of coming into consciousness; we usually move through this passage so quickly that we bring no awareness to it at all. That morning, as I awoke, my head was facing west so that my eyes opened across the Rio Grande Valley to the Jemez Mountains, and this moment of awakening spread before me just as the valley did. Rather than passing through it quickly, I seemed to unfold into a world of timelessness, and in that grand expanse I felt the unnameable flow of life that links me all my way back to the moment of Creation *through my ancestors*—through the ugly rapings and the musket shots and tattered flesh back through the weddings and crocheted lace and birthings in dank stone rooms; the witch burnings, the scientific theories; all the glorious and all the horrendous, the jubilant, the twisted, the unspeakable; back through the cave paintings and the animal furs and the night chants, including the hairy beasts, the shore creatures, seaweed and plankton, lightning; me, all the way back to Creation.

What had previously prevented me from embracing my lineage—the inherent uprootedness of my people, the lack of tradition passed down to me, my righteous sense of disgust at history, the violence my father had perpetrated—fell into a new place, subsumed now by the vast flow of life. I was left not without my previous awareness of and sense of responsibility for my ancestry, but buoyed now by something bigger: an almost boundless pool of vitality that seemed to flow up from the Earth through my heart into my arteries. I had the sense that morning that my blood grew thicker. The chronic lack of rootedness I had known before had been a constellation of bodily feelings: a thinness of blood, a fragility of the nervous system, a constriction, a fear—all feelings that now faded into the past. The spirits of my ancestors had called out to me; I had heard them.

I now live with a sense of interconnectedness not just with the junipers and hawks alive today, but with all the ancestors who ever lived. As anthropologist Joan Halifax describes this shift, "Ancestors and nature-kin are again in the sacred circle."[8]

All My Spirits

Another challenging leap in our reclamation of full earthly communion takes us to the rest of the spirit world and to the nonordinary states of consciousness that are required to bridge the perceptual gap between ourselves and the beings of the invisible world. "Judging by folklore and myths," writes Scott Russell Sanders, "this is a perennial human desire, to converse with our neighbors in their separate dialects—to speak bear with bear, oak with oak, flint with flint—and once in a great while to leap into the universal language and hear and be heard by the creator."[9]

To indigenous people, communicating with the Creator is an accepted aspect of life. As ethnographer Richard Erdoes explains of the ghost dance of the late nineteenth century, "A dancer falls down in a trance, dying, and then coming to life again. Upon awakening, men and women [speak] of having traveled to the Moon or to the Morning Star, coming back with 'Star Flesh' in their clenched fists, flesh of the planets which had been turned into strange rocks."[10] To us, the prospect of such activity is presented as weird, unreal, and impractical. Ever since the witch burnings destroyed the last strongholds of nature-based practitioners in the west, the realm of nonordinary states of consciousness has been shunted into the lowly occult. And yet, despite suppression, nonordinary states of consciousness persist.

Some of us pursue the experience in occult practices; for others, it seems to come knocking unexpectedly on our perceptual doors. This unexpected summoning is what happened to Marc Kasky, longtime ecologist and the director of San

Francisco's Fort Mason Center.[11] Every summer Kasky travels to the High Sierra for a two-week solo into the wilds. In 1992 he hiked to high-mountain Moraine Lake. As Kasky describes the night of his summons, "Before I turned in, I was sitting in front of my tent looking upward at the darkening sky. I let my field of vision drop down to the tree line riding the horizon of the mountain, then down to the mountain itself, then to the lake which was by this time shiny and black, down across the lake to the rocks on the beach, finally to my own feet. Everything was quiet; no wind, no animal sounds. I felt totally open in my heart and totally connected to it all."

Kasky went to sleep outside his tent and, by his report, was awakened in the middle of the night. At the edge of his campsite stood a hairy creature, humanlike in shape, about five feet eight inches tall, staring right at him. The creature gestured to him to follow. "I wasn't afraid," Kasky now relates. "But I was hesitant—and nervous about wandering around in the dark in a rocky area. I declined, and fell back asleep."

The next morning, while hiking in nearby Sky Parlor Meadow, Kasky had an insight as unexpected as the creature's visitation: this being was a messenger from the spirit world whose purpose was to invite him in. Then he wondered: could it be that as a culture, we too are hesitant, not quite ready, but awakening to the possibilities?

Anthropologist Felicitas Goodman works with Europeans and Euro-Americans who are ready. During the course of her research on spirit-inducing religious trance, Goodman unearthed thirty body postures found in the art and ritual practices of eastern, western esoteric, and nature-based cultures.[12] When used in appropriate ceremonial settings, these postures can induce powerful visions that reiterate the themes of spiritual connectedness, life and death, healing and illness, woman and man, sacred and profane that are found over and over again among nature-based peoples. Now in her eighties, Goodman conducts six-day trainings in these trance methods at her Cuyamungue Institute in northern New Mexico. During these trainings, group trances take place twice a day in the kiva for the purpose of creating a collective vision that the group celebrates on the last night. When participants are not in the kiva, they are constructing masks and costumes for this celebration.

As one of her students, the eco-feminist Johanna Maybury, describes this experience, "One year during this final night, we were all standing on the special court where the event takes place, and we were holding hands in a circle. Felicitas was, as always, wearing her grand buffalo costume and as jubilant as ever. I will never forget: she said to us, 'This is the way it used to be in Old Europe. *This is our tradition*.' "[13]

What do such endeavors have to do with solving systemic psychological and ecological problems? Why does a book proposing a linkage between psychological dysfunction and ecological disaster veer in the direction of altered states of consciousness? Just as trust and individuality are crucial qualities to develop in our effort to retrieve sanity, so are these glimpses. Nonordinary states of consciousness provide the psychic bridge between a generalized sense of relatedness to the natural world, the purpose of a people, the challenges of personal development, and the details of day-to-day existence. They have evolved within our psyches through some thirty-five thousand generations and more—not as some weird violation of daily consciousness, but as an essential mode of participation in the elliptical nature of our lives on Earth.

The role of the medicine man or woman may offer us some insight. This healer is the spiritual guide who typically resides in nature-based culture. Anthropologists use the term *shaman* to describe this person when, in fact, the role may be embodied in a singular individual—say a !Kung healer, or may be expanded to include any tribal member—a sun dancer, for instance—who engages in a particular practice. Halifax describes the shaman as the "wounded healer"[14]—the reluctant adventurer whose life unexpectedly presents the challenge of illness and cracks him open to the full round of possibilities of psychic reality, or the conscious adventurer who purposefully inflicts trauma upon herself in order to open to these same possibilities. When the participant forges a conscious integration of the experience, the journey to the spirit world is a success.

We face an ironic twist. Here we have an entire civilization of people wounded as profoundly as any spiritual leader from New Guinea or the Arctic Circle. As we attempt to make sense of our predicament by intermingling social analysis, psychological understanding, and the cultural knowledge of indigenous peoples, we cannot help but wonder if we inhabitants of today's society might actually have the capability to transform ourselves into wounded healers. Granted, few of us enter into the trauma imposed by our civilization with either conscious choice or a welcome attitude toward the challenge of post-trauma integration. Granted, the early onset of the traumatization process prevents us from developing the trust and centeredness that medicine people have presumably had the opportunity to develop. Granted, many of us then endure childhood violence that further truncates any sustenance we might milk from our early environs. Granted, the woundings are continuous in the daily fare of crime, racial violence, technological disasters, economic hardships, AIDS, cancer, wars. Granted, our culture offers no tradition to guide or make sense of such an integrative challenge.

Yet let us consider that while we certainly would never have wished for this predicament, it nonetheless presses us toward our wildest imaginings. The traumatized person who accomplishes the work of recovery has the potential of becoming *more* integrated and *more* aware than the person who has endured no blatant trauma and has never had to piece together a shattered psyche. The acquired talents and resources of medicine people verify this potential, as do the importance of their job and the honoring they receive for doing it. The task is to dwell in the land of the spirits—and then to return to the Earth world, bringing back the information and wisdom learned. The task is a sacred undertaking: it is to inform, guide, and inspire the people. Perhaps the most well known example of a vision informing a people comes to us from the Oglala Lakota medicine man Black Elk. During a childhood illness, Black Elk had a magnificent dream about the restoration of dignity to his people. In the dream the Grandfathers of the Flaming Rainbow Teepee gave him a cup to catch rainwater from the west, a peace pipe from the north, a flowering branch from the south, and a fan-petaled herb of healing from the east, and they showed him a great ceremony involving these gifts. Black Elk told no one about the dream. When he was seventeen years of age, though, he endured a series of paralyzing anxiety attacks. A medicine man advised him, "For a person who has a vision, you do not get the power of your vision until you perform it on earth for the people to see."[15]

Contemplating the purpose of the spirit-communication skills she is learning as a student of Goodman's work, therapist Luisa Kolker perceives her trance studies as a training. "My body is continually refining itself, becoming like a tuning fork or a transmitter," she says. "This is a training, a preparation. . . ."[16] For what? Is it possible that we westerners, *because* of our woundings, might possess the capability of providing vision that could inform, guide, and inspire us toward the creation of a sane and ecological future?

15

Our Wildest Dreams

We never left—never left our true, real context. . . . We left that context only in our fevered imagination. It all began as an act of imagination, an illusory image—most fundamentally an image of fear—and so the corrective process must likewise begin with an image. Let us relearn what hunter-gatherers knew to the core of their being, that this place and its processes (even in our death) always takes care of us—that Homo's citizenship and errand rest not with any creed or state but with "that star's substance from which he had arisen."

—CALVIN MARTIN,
In the Spirit of the Earth

I set out in this book to draw a relationship between the deluge of psychological dysfunctions among us and the ecological crisis besieging our planet. I found that I could not adequately reveal this linkage without diagnosing the fundamental pathology of our western world, and to counter this frightening vision, I offered a glimpse of sanity in nature-based culture. After making such an exploration, I feel we are left with a distinction whose clarity rivals the lucidity of a paleolithic pool: a distinction between what, given its myriad variations, is universal and what, given its knee-jerk predictability, is pathological.

Fortunately for us, universal qualities, concerns, and urges manage to peek through the most corrosive violations of our humanity. Against the horrific backdrop of a technocracy charging headlong toward the synthesization of virtually all reality, we may thank the spirits that we can still love our families, feel affection for animals, and be left spellbound by snow-peaked mountains. The point I am making is a rather grand and, at the same time, simple one. Our lives upon this Earth are part of a vast, magnificent, and unfathomable whole. A man's passion for his work is inextricably intertwined with his communion with the mountain of his ancestors; if you chase him from the mountain, you tamper with the passion. When the patterns of livelihood connecting our nomadic ancestors to the web of life were broken in one seemingly minor way—domestication—the whole was shattered into a thousand fragments.

Healing is a process of rounding up all the fragments and reconciling them. There are among us today people of the most admirable intention who still, naively, fracture the whole—believing that the plastic can still be produced, that the high-tech armies and electromagnetics are here forever, that mass technological society is a fait accompli. According to such thinking, healing is a compromise. What healing we need for adjusting to our technological encasement can be accomplished by support groups of one sort or another, through some neo-entrepreneurship or New Age workshop, via "rational guidance" of technological development. Our hearts will somehow change; we will somehow learn to be kind. . . . Given that the nuclear armies and global electromagnetics are here now, *any* intervention that moves us toward healing is crucial. But ultimately, authentic recovery from western civilization must include every fragment of our collective shattering—not just our self-esteem and where we dump the garbage, but how we structure our communities, how we speak and make decisions, what artifacts we create and who creates them, what we eat, how we dream, who we think we are, how we relate to the mountain of our ancestors, how we bring our children into the world, and how all these facets of our lives fit together.

The question I hope I have raised is this: *what does it mean to be a human being?* This is a question that has been asked again and again throughout our history. Originally nature-based people answered it by living as humble participants in the all-embracing cycle of sycamore, blueberry, rainfall, and spirit. About ten thousand years ago, western peoples began to answer the question with an unprecedented dedication to managed fecundity, and today the urgency to meaning is translated into the seeming predictability of technological encasement. In the last analysis, the answer to our question of meaning lies in the nature of who we are. Throughout our time on Earth, there have been swallows flying across the clouds, dandelion puffs carried by the wind and dropped to the soil, furry creatures and slippery beings roaming the land, a moon that waxes and wanes in the night. Our psyches too are natural worlds, mirrors and dreams of this wildness around us; this reality is our essence.

Some may say that this is an extremely radical vision, perhaps too radical. The word *radical* means "original, fundamental, reaching to the center or ultimate source," becoming again who we are. As a person who has struggled nearly my entire life with the pain and disorientation of traumatic stress, I accept no partial dysfunctions for myself, no kind-of healings, no halfway recoveries. Always, even before I understood the source of my suffering, I intended to heal 100 percent. Likewise, the guiding impetus behind this book is this urge to wholeness which, as we know from both our personal and collective histories, will not quiet down until wholeness is once again ours.

Perhaps you believe that the "benefits" of technological society are worth the "trade-offs." Or you are boggled by the fact that the survival of millions of people depends on the delivery and communications strategies currently in place. Perhaps you feel it would be silly or impossible to "go back."

I offer you a forward-looking challenge. No one has yet conjured a coherent vision of what a deeply wounded humanity living upon a deeply ravaged planet, having long since surpassed the limits of sustainability, might become. When media entrepreneur Ted Turner funded a competition to find a fictional work demonstrating a plan for sustainability, ten thousand manuscripts poured in. And yet, reports Turner, "we did not have one plausible treatise on how we could get to a sustainable, peaceful future."[1] I do not claim to be the first to offer such a vision. I do, however, know that given our current state of psychic and ecological dislocation, we remain ill prepared to make the pressing decisions concerning mental health, ecological practices, technological development, economic policy, and education. To make such decisions, and make them with intelligence, we must know our full humanity and a fully vital relationship to the Earth; we must reside in the primal matrix.

To those of you who harbor doubt, I offer a personal challenge as well: to embark upon this process of recovery from western civilization, to begin to reclaim those parts of yourself and the Earth that have been lost. Then, when you have attained even the slightest glimpse of this terrain, try to refute a vision asserting that we be allowed to heal 100 percent. And remember, turn over in your mind what humanities professor Annette Kolodny refers to as "the nagging fact of Euro-American and native relations":[2] on the whole, the native peoples of this Earth have never longed to join the dominant civilization; they have always preferred to be left alone to live their own ways.

The Oracle

The Kogi are an indigenous people of the Sierra Nevada of Colombia, the last intact population of preconquest Mesoamericans. Four centuries ago, the Spanish conquistadors slaughtered the ancestors of these Indian peoples—burning and looting their homelands, gunning them down, setting vicious dogs on them, slicing off their ears to get gold jewelry. The great warrior Cuchacique was dragged by two horses through the streets, his body quartered, and his head, arms, and torso put on public display.

The Kogi Nation that exists today was pieced together by a desperate collection of survivors who fled into the mountains to form a subsistence society. Today this society is guided by a spiritual priesthood, the "Mamas," whose self-appointed job is to continue the traditional role of the peoples of this terrain: to balance the Earth. Believing themselves to be the guardians of all life, the Kogi follow a morality whose central concern is the health of the planet. They call the place where they live the Heart of the World; they call themselves the Elder Brothers; they call Christopher Columbus and everyone who came after him—all the conquerors, gold diggers, armies, bankers, guerrillas, tomb looters, bureaucrats, miners, drug lords, prostitutes, archaeologists, anthropologists, and tourists—the Younger Brother.

In 1988, after successfully hiding from the civilized world for over four centuries, the Kogi made an unprecedented decision. They decided to speak to the Younger Brother about the fate of the Earth *just once*, and then to return to their hidden world. They accomplished this momentous mission with the help of a British historian and journalist named Alan Ereira who, with a BBC film crew, was briefly allowed to enter the forbidden land of the Elder Brother.

The content of the Kogi message will come as no surprise; the surprise lies in the fact that they thought to deliver it at all. The Kogi's conclusions come in part from observation of the ecological deterioration of the water, air, flora, and fauna of the Sierra Nevada, in part from observation of the activities of the urban dwellers below, in part by spiritual divination. The message given for the BBC film resulted from an actual water oracle, the priests asking, "How should we speak to the world?" and the answer coming:

> From the beginning in Colombia
> everything, everything remained as it always was
> among us,
> the native people;
> the same belief,
> the same mask,
> the same dance.
> Everything well organized,
> in order,
> a terrace for every animal.
>   . . .
>
> But Younger Brother came from another country
> and immediately he saw gold
> and immediately he began to rob.
> There was golden images,
> golden oracles.
> The Mama prophesied with golden bowls,
> he had a golden tuma,
> he had everything
> and Younger Brother took it all to another country.
>
> Now the Mama grows sad,
> he feels weak.
> He says that the earth is decaying.
> The earth is losing its strength
> because they have taken away much petrol,
> coal,
> many minerals.
>   . . .
>
> So the earth today catches diseases of all kinds.
> The animals die.
> The trees dry up.
> People fall ill.

Many illnesses will appear,
and there will be no cure for them.
Why?

Because Younger Brother is among us,
Younger Brother is violating
the basic foundation of the world's law.
A total violation.
Robbing.
Ransacking.
Building highways,
extracting petrol,
minerals.
. . .

So the Mamas say,
"Please BBC
no one else should come here,
no more ransacking
because the earth wants to collapse,
the earth grows weak,
we must protect it,
we must respect it,
because he does not respect the earth,
because he does not respect it."
. . .

The earth feels.
They take out the petrol,
it feels pain there.
So the earth sends out sickness.
There will be many medicines,
drugs,
but in the end the drugs will not be of any use,
neither will the medicine be of any use.

The Mamas say that this tale must be learnt
by the Younger Brother.[3]

Praise Creation

To learn this tale brings us face to face with our passion to bring
about change, and as it happens, the last step of every system
that addresses psychological recovery concerns action. The
consciousness-raising groups women engaged in during the
1970s launched the bookstores, womens' shelters, rape crisis
centers, books, films, and legislation of the women's movement.
The recovery process from childhood abuse encourages survivors
to invent ways to bring justice into the world, while perpetrators
are required to make meaningful amends with those they have
injured. Step Twelve of Alcoholics Anonymous states: "Having
had a spiritual awakening as a result of these steps, we tried to
carry this message to others, and to practice these principles in all
our affairs."[4]

Action is a merging of our convictions about what must be
done in the world with our sense of spiritual connectedness. I
remember, only a few months after my discovery of childhood
trauma, walking the meandering ribbon of road between
Tesuque and Santa Fe. Suddenly I was seized by a bodily feeling.
Suddenly, it was as if every cell of my being was lining itself up for
the purpose of my life: to bring healing into the world, to stop
the pain, the trauma, the disease. At once I felt linked to all of
life's flow; to all people, past, present, and future; to all creatures,
to all land—knowing my place as a healer-warrior on this Earth.
At this same moment, a vision revealed itself, a vision that
corresponded exactly to this feeling I was having. I saw an old
native woman wrinkled with wisdom, maybe Hopi, up on the
mesa at Oraibi, the sand stinging in the wind. She was absolutely
sure of her mission, more sure than I had ever known a human
being to be, unstoppable in her conviction.

"Let your life be a friction against the machine," wrote Henry
David Thoreau in 1854.[5] "There is a time when the operation of

the machine becomes so odious, makes you so sick at heart that you can't take part, you can't even passively take part," bellowed Mario Savio at a rally in Berkeley, California, during the Free Speech Movement in 1964, "and you've got to put your bodies upon the gears and upon the wheels, upon the levers, upon all the apparatus and you've got to make it stop. And you've got to indicate to the people who run it, to the people who own it, that unless you're free, the machine will be prevented from working at all."[6] "It is imperative," writes educator Gloria Orenstein, "that we go about the task of creating an alternative society, and a culture that is interconnected with nature *now*."[7]

To bring about our wildest dreams, there is personal healing to do. There are community enmities to mend, families to nourish, children to whom we must teach the ways of the natural world. There are daily acts we can engage in: turning off the television, gathering and eating the dandelions instead of spraying them with pesticides, playing music together, walking to work, democratizing our meetings, celebrating our family gatherings. There are research studies to launch, educational approaches to invent, ecological practices to institute—and more Earth-restoration efforts than we can imagine. There is political work to accomplish, too—*much* political work. Finally, there is ceremony to perform, for the ceremonies we create will shape the politics we engage in, the dreams we live, and the meaning of our lives.

Haudenosaunee statesman Leon Shenandoah tells a story in which all the creatures of the world gather in council to clarify the jobs they each are to perform in the service of Creation.[8] One by one, they step forward. The beaver is here to look after the wetlands and to monitor how the streams flow through the mountains. The worm is here to burrow through the earth so that the roots of plants may find air and nutrients. The deer is here to slip through the woodlands, to watch what is happening. The council is progressing well—but one poor creature stands in the background, uncertain of his role. This is the human. At last a man steps forward and haltingly addresses the assembly. "We are confused," he says. "What is the purpose of human beings?" The animals and the plants, the insects and the trees—all are surprised. "Don't you *know*?! It's so . . . obvious!!" "No," replies the man, "we need you to tell us." And the other creatures of the world respond, "Your purpose is to glory in it all. Your job is to praise Creation."

All nature-based cultures praise Creation. Some do so with daily personal practices such as waking with the dawn to thank the spirits. Others dance into the night to maintain balanced relations with the forces of the natural world, while still others perform tribal ceremonies for the purpose of keeping the world going.

As Shenandoah explains, "Our religion is all about thanking the Creator. . . . We thank Him for the world and every animal and plant in it. We thank Him for everything that exists. We don't take it for granted that a tree's just there. We thank the Creator for that tree. If we don't thank Him, maybe the Creator will take that tree away. That's what our ceremonies are about, that's why they're important. . . . We pray for the harmony of the whole world. We believe if we didn't do our ceremonies in the Longhouse the world would come to an end. It's our ceremonies that hold the world together. Some people may not believe that, they may laugh at it, but it's true. The Creator wants to be thanked."[9]

We westerners have long since discontinued a communal practice of praising Creation and in so doing, of aligning ourselves with the continuity of life on Earth. We are called now, as never before, to act upon our understanding of dysfunction and our urge toward wholeness.

I have imagined that the time will come when we will take up the purpose of human life once again. I have imagined magnificent ceremonies in which, once again, we will glory in it all, join together with the indigenous people of the Earth to offer thanksgiving, resume our task of helping to keep the world going. Until the time comes when these ceremonies unify our lives once again, we each, alongside our families and friends, can initiate our recovery from western civilization with a simple but radical act: *praise Creation.*

You call it wild, but it wasn't really wild, it was free.

—LEON SHENANDOAH, quoted in
Wisdomkeepers

Notes

Preface

1. Chellis Glendinning, *Waking Up in the Nuclear Age* (Philadelphia: New Society Publishers, 1987).
2. Chellis Glendinning, *When Technology Wounds: The Human Consequences of Progress* (New York: Morrow, 1990).
3. David Abram, "The Ecology of Magic," *Orion* 10, no. 3 (Summer 1991): 43.
4. William Devall and George Sessions, *Deep Ecology* (Layton, Utah: Peregrine Smith, 1985), ix.
5. Lewis Mumford, "Prologue to Our Time," *The New Yorker*, 10 March 1975.

1. People and Nature

1. David Haenke, telephone conversation, 6 August 1990.
2. Carole Roberts, telephone conversation, 19 February 1991.
3. Jean Liedloff, *The Continuum Concept* (Reading, Mass.: Addison-Wesley, 1985), 74–75.
4. Russell Thornton, *American Indian Holocaust and Survival: A Population History Since 1492* (Norman, Okla.: University of Oklahoma Press, 1987), 25–36; and George Russell, "A Quincentennial Map of American Indian History" (Phoenix: Thunderbird Enterprises, 1992).
5. Ben Winton, "Navajos, Cherokee Largest Tribes," *Albuquerque Journal*, 19 November 1992, A7.
6. Eugene Linden, "Lost Tribes, Lost Knowledge," *Time*, 23 September 1991, 48.
7. Julian Lang, telephone conversation, 5 June 1992.

8. Douglas Cardinal and Jeannette Armstrong, *The Native Creative Process* (Penticton, Canada: Theytus Books, 1991), 12.
9. Jerry Mander, telephone conversation, 20 August 1991.

2. Primal Matrix

1. Lindsay Holt, telephone conversation, Santa Fe, N. Mex., 16 February 1992.
2. Frances Harwood, telephone conversation, Tesuque, N. Mex., 1 September 1992.
3. Jean Liedloff, *The Continuum Concept* (Reading, Mass.: Addison-Wesley, 1985), 10.
4. Stanislav Grof, *The Adventure of Self-Discovery* (Albany, N.Y.: State University of New York Press, 1988), 7–10.
5. Ibid., 3–7.
6. Ibid., 37–39.
7. Erik Erikson, *The Life Cycle Completed* (New York: W. W. Norton, 1982), 55.
8. Liedloff, *The Continuum Concept*, 22–23.
9. Jeannette Armstrong, "The Ones Who Are Dream and Land Together," *Elmwood Quarterly* 7, no. 3 (Fall Equinox 1991): 3.
10. Paul Shepard, *Nature and Madness* (San Francisco: Sierra Club Books, 1982), 7.
11. Morris Berman, *The Re-enchantment of the World* (New York: Bantam, 1987), 2.
12. John Mohawk, conversation, Rhinebeck, N.Y., 8 August 1992.
13. Paula Gunn Allen, "The Sacred Hoop: A Contemporary Indian Perspective on American Indian Literature," in Jerome Rothenberg and Diane Rothenberg, eds., *Symposium of the Whole* (Berkeley: University of California Press, 1983), 175.
14. Elizabeth Roberts and Elias Amidon, eds., *Earth Prayers* (San Francisco, HarperSanFrancisco, 1991), p. 70.
15. Calvin Martin, *In the Spirit of the Earth* (Baltimore: Johns Hopkins University Press, 1992), 85–86.
16. Liedloff, *The Continuum Concept*, 81.
17. Dorothy Eggan, "The General Problem of Hopi Adjustment," in Clyde Kluckhorn and Henry Murray, eds., *Personality in Nature, Society and Culture* (New York: Alfred Knopf, 1949), 225.

18. Brian Morris, *Forest Traders: A Socio-Economic Study of the Hill Pandaram* (London: Athlone Press, 1982), 113, 129.
19. Anne Wilson Schaef, *Co-Dependence* (New York: Harper and Row, 1986), 44–45.
20. Liedloff, *The Continuum Concept*, 78.
21. James Woodburn, "Hunters and Gatherers Today and Reconstruction of the Past," in Ernest Geller, ed., *Soviet and Western Anthropology* (London: Duckworth, 1980).
22. Liedloff, *The Continuum Concept*, 92–94.
23. Morris, *Forest Traders*, 130.
24. Lorna Marshall, *The !Kung of Nyae Nyae* (Cambridge: Harvard University Press, 1976).
25. Shepard, *Nature and Madness*, 34.
26. Grof, *The Adventure of Self-Discovery*, sec. 1.
27. Allen, "The Sacred Hoop," 183.
28. Greg Cajete, "Learning about Indian Science," *Elmwood Newsletter* 5, no. 1 (Spring Equinox 1989): 5.
29. Allen, "The Sacred Hoop," 184.
30. Cajete, "Learning about Indian Science," 5.
31. Allen, "The Sacred Hoop," 183.
32. Larry Emerson, conversation, Shiprock, N. Mex., 10 February 1991.

3. A Lesson in Earth Civics

1. Stanley Diamond, *In Search of the Primitive* (New Brunswick, N.J.: Transaction Books, 1974), 143.
2. Frances Harwood, conversation, Roosevelt, Tex., 18 May 1992.
3. Quoted in Robert Dahl and Edward Tufte, *Size and Democracy* (Stanford, Calif.: Stanford University Press, 1973), 111.
4. Kirkpatrick Sale, foreword to Leopold Kohr, *The Breakdown of Nations* (New York: E. P. Dutton, 1978), ix–x.
5. Joseph Birdsell, "Some Predictions for the Pleistocene Based in Equilibrium Systems among Recent Hunter-Gatherers," in Richard Lee and Irven DeVore, eds., *Man the Hunter* (Chicago: Aldine Atherton, 1968), 11.
6. Peter Nabokov, *Native American Testimony* (New York: Viking, 1991),

4; M. A. Baumhoff, "Ecological Determinants of Aboriginal California Populations," *University of California Publications in American Archaeology and Ethnology*, 49, 2 (1963) 155–236; and J. H. Stewart, *Theory of
Culture Change* (Urbana, Illinois: University of Illinois Press, 1955).

7. Birdsell, "Some Predictions for the Pleistocene," 11.

8. Colin Turnbull, *The Forest People* (New York: Doubleday Anchor,
1962), chap. 6.

9. Jerry Mander, *In the Absence of the Sacred* (San Francisco: Sierra Club
Books, 1991), 230–35. *See also* Robert Venables, "American Indian
Influences on the American Founding Fathers," in Oren Lyons and
John Mohawk, eds., *Exiled in the Land of the Free* (Santa Fe, N. Mex.:
Clear Light Publishers, 1992), 73–124.

10. Dolores LaChapelle, *Earth Wisdom* (Los Angeles: L.A. Guild of Tudor
Press, 1978), 81.

11. Frances Huxley, conversation, Santa Fe, N. Mex., 4 March 1992.

12. Huxley, conversation.

13. Peter Wilson, *The Domestication of the Human Species* (New Haven,
Conn.: Yale University Press, 1988), 33.

14. Cited in Mander, *Absence of the Sacred*, 254.

15. A. Kent MacDougall, "Americans: Life in the Fast Lane/The Harried
Society," *Los Angeles Times*, 17–19 April 1983.

16. Frederick McCarthy and Margaret McArthur, "The Food Quest and
the Time Factor in Aboriginal Economic Life," in C. P. Mountford,
ed., *Records of the Australian-American Scientific Expedition to Arnhem
Land* (Melbourne: Melbourne University Press, 1960), vol. 2, *Anthropology and Nutrition*, 145–94.

17. Richard Lee, "What Hunters Do for a Living or How to Make Out on
Scarce Resources," in Lee and DeVore, *Man the Hunter*, 37.

18. Clive Ponting, "Historical Perspectives on Sustainable Development,"
Environment 32, no. 9 (November 1990): 4–5.

19. Marshall Sahlins, *Stone Age Economics* (New York: Aldine De Gruyter,
1972), 36.

20. Mark Nathan Cohen, *Health and the Rise of Civilization* (New Haven,
Conn.: Yale University Press, 1989), 75–98.

21. Lee, "What Hunters Do," 33.

22. Cited in MacDougall, "Americans."

23. McCarthy and McArthur, "The Food Quest," 145–94; Lee, "What
Hunters Do," 30–48; Richard Lee, "!Kung Bushman Subsistence: An

Input-Output Analysis," in A. P. Vayda, ed., *Ecological Studies in Cultural Anthropology* (New York: Natural History Press, 1969), 47–79; and J. Metz et al., "Iron, Folate, and Vitamin B12 Nutrition in a Hunter-Gatherer People: A Study of !Kung Bushmen," *American Journal of Clinical Nutrition* 24 (1971): 229–42.

24. Cohen, *Health*, 98–102; Francis Black, "Infectious Diseases in Primitive Societies," *Science* 187 (1975): 515–18; Ivan Polunin, "The Medical Natural History of Malayan Aborigines," *Medical Journal of Malaysia* 8 (1972): 55–174; Roberto Baruzzi and L. Franco, "Amerindians of Brazil," in H. C. Trowell and D. P. Burkitt, eds., *Western Diseases, Their Emergence and Prevention* (London: Edward Arnold, 1981), 138–53; and H. H. Draper, "Nutrition Studies: The Aboriginal Eskimo Diet" in P. L. Jamison, ed., *Eskimos of Northwestern Alaska* (Stroudsberg, Pa.: USIBP, 1978), 139–61.

25. Samuel Hahnemann, *The Chronic Diseases* (New Delhi: Jain, 1975).

26. Cited in Mark Hertsgaard, "Still Ticking," *Mother Jones*, March/April 1993, 20–23.

27. United Nations, Secretariat, "World Population Prospects Beyond Year 2000," New York, 16 May 1973.

28. Cited in Craig Comstock, "Envisioning a Sustainable World Population," *Elmwood Quarterly* 7, no. 3 (Fall Equinox 1991): 5.

29. Ponting, "Historical Perspectives on Sustainable Development," 6.

30. Fekri Hassan, *Demographic Archaeology* (New York: Academic Press, 1981), 208.

31. Ponting, "Historical Perspectives on Sustainable Development," 6.

32. M. Konner and C. Worthman, "Nursing Frequencies, Gonadal Function, and Birth-Spacing among !Kung Hunter-Gatherers," *Science* 207 (1988): 788–91; Richard Lee, *The !Kung San: Men, Women and Work in a Foraging Society* (Cambridge: Cambridge University Press, 1979), 328–30; W. H. Billewicz, "The Timing of Post Partum Menstruation and Breast-Feeding," *Journal of Biosocial Science* 11 (1979): 141–51; and W. H. Mosley, "The Effects of Nutrition on Natural Fertility" (Paper presented at Seminar on Natural Fertility, Institut National d'Etudes Demographiques, Paris, 1977).

33. Lee, *The !Kung San*, 329.

34. Lee, *The !Kung San*, 312; R. E. Frisch, "Critical Weight at Menarche: Initiation of the Adolescent Growth Spurt and Control of Puberty," in M. M. Brumbach et al., eds., *Control of Onset of Puberty* (New York:

Wiley, 1974), 403–23; G. R. Bentley, "Hunter-Gatherer Energetics and Fertility: A Reassessment of the !Kung San," *Human Ecology* 13, no. 1 (1985): 79–104; J. B. McArthur et al., "Hypothalamic Amenorrhea in Runners of Normal Body Composition," *Endocrine Research Communications* 7, no. 1 (1980): 13–25; M. Shangold et al., "The Relationship between Long Distance Running and Plasma Progesterone, and Luteal Phase Length," *Fertility and Sterility* 31, no. 2 (1979): 130–33; and R. Frisch and J. MacArthur, "Menstrual Cycles: Fatness as a Determinant of Minimum Weight or Height Necessary for Their Maintenance or Onset," *Science* 185 (1974): 949–51.

35. Sahlins, *Stone Age Economics*, 41.

4. Original Trauma

1. Robert Romanyshyn, *Technology as Symptom and Dream* (London: Routledge, 1989), 33.
2. Samuel Edgerton, *The Renaissance Rediscovery of Linear Perspective* (New York: Harper and Row, 1976), 9–10.
3. Paul Shepard, *Nature and Madness* (San Francisco: Sierra Club Books, 1982), chap. 2.
4. Susan Griffin, *Woman and Nature* (New York: Harper Colophon, 1978), 95–96.
5. Ovid *Metamorphoses* 1. Translated in Arthur Lovejoy and George Boas, *Primitivism and Related Ideas in Antiquity* (Baltimore: Johns Hopkins University Press, 1935), 46.
6. Terry Kellogg, "The Roots of Addiction" (Lecture presented at the Institute for Integral Development, Colorado Springs, Colo., August 1991).
7. Kai Erikson, *Everything in Its Path* (New York: Simon and Schuster, 1976), 255.
8. Sigmund Freud, *Civilization and Its Discontents* (New York: W. W. Norton, 1961).
9. Samuel Hahnemann, *The Chronic Diseases* (New Delhi: Jain, 1975).
10. Starhawk, *Dreaming the Dark* (Boston: Beacon Press, 1982), 183–219; and Johanna Maybury, conversation with, Santa Fe, N. Mex., 1 June 1990.

5. Domestication

1. James Lovelock, *Healing Gaia* (New York: Harmony Books, 1991), 156.
2. Lionel Tiger and Robin Fox, *The Imperial Animal* (New York: Henry Holt, 1989), 126.
3. Jared Diamond, "The Worst Mistake in the History of the Human Race," *Discover*, May 1987, 64.
4. Charlene Spretnak, *States of Grace* (San Francisco: Harper San Francisco, 1991), 129.
5. Paul Shepard, *Nature and Madness* (San Francisco: Sierra Club Books, 1982), 64–66.
6. For a comprehensive discussion of theories of the origins of agriculture, see Fekri Hassan, *Demographic Archaeology* (New York: Academic Press, 1981), chap. 13.
7. E. N. Anderson, "On the Social Context of Early Food Production," *Current Anthropology* 27, no. 3 (1986): 262–63.
8. Shepard, *Nature and Madness*, 52.
9. Raymond Williams, *The Country and the City* (Oxford: Oxford University Press, 1973), 171.
10. Calvin Martin, *In the Spirit of the Earth* (Baltimore: Johns Hopkins University Press, 1992), 22–23.
11. Suzan Harjo, conversation, Albuquerque, N. Mex. 6 July 1992.
12. Robert Jay Lifton, *Death in Life: Survivors of Hiroshima* (New York: Basic Books, 1982), 54, 305, 400–401.
13. Chaim Shatan, "Have You Hugged a Vietnam Veteran Today?" in William Kelly, ed., *Post-Traumatic Stress Disorder and the War Veteran Patient* (New York: Brunner Mazel, 1985), 13.
14. Sigmund Freud, *Civilization and Its Discontents* (New York: W. W. Norton, 1961), 92.
15. Robert Jay Lifton, *The Broken Connection* (New York: Simon and Schuster, 1979).
16. Marija Gimbutas, *The Civilization of the Goddess* (San Francisco: Harper Collins, 1991); Marija Gimbutas, *The Language of the Goddess* (San Francisco: Harper and Row, 1989); Riane Eisler, *The Chalice and the Blade* (San Francisco: Harper and Row, 1987); and Merlin Stone, *When God Was a Woman* (New York: Harcourt Brace Jovanovich, 1976).

17. Colin Renfrew, *Archaeology and Language* (Cambridge: Cambridge University Press, 1987).

18. Margaret Ehrenberg, *Women in Prehistory* (Norman, Okla.: University of Oklahoma Press, 1989), 77.

19. Frederick Engels, *The Origins of the Family, Private Property and the State* (New York: International, 1972); K. Sacks, "Engels Re-visited: Women, the Organization of Production and Private Property," in M. Rosaldo and L. Lamphere, eds., *Woman, Culture, and Society* (Stanford, Calif.: Stanford University Press, 1974); R. Reiter, "The Search for Origins: Unraveling the Threads of Gender Hierarchy," *Critique of Anthropology* 2 (1978): 5–24; and N. Quinn, "Anthropological Studies on Women's Status," *Annual Review of Anthropology* 6 (1977): 181–225.

20. Ehrenberg, *Women in Prehistory*, 106–7.

21. Fekri Hassan, *Demographic Archaeology* (New York: Academic Press, 1981), 221; cited in Donald O. Henry, *From Foraging to Agriculture* (Philadelphia: University of Pennsylvania Press, 1989), 41.

22. Henry, *From Foraging to Agriculture*, 23–24, 41–44.

23. Henry, *From Foraging to Agriculture*, 43; Ehrenberg, *Women in Prehistory*, 89; and Lewis Binford, *An Archaeological Perspective* (New York: Seminar Press, 1972).

24. Henry, *From Foraging to Agriculture*, 43; Richard Lee, "!Kung Bushmen Subsistence: An Input-Output Analysis," in A. P. Vayda, ed., *Environment and Cultural Behavior* (New York: Natural History Press, 1969), 47–49; and M. Harris, *Cannibals and Kings* (New York: Random House, 1977).

25. Henry, *From Foraging to Agriculture*, 43; and Ehrenberg, *Women in Prehistory*, 89.

26. Ehrenberg, *Women in Prehistory*, 103.

27. Clive Ponting, "Historical Perspectives on Sustainable Development," *Environment* 32, no. 9 (November 1990): 6.

28. Robert Carneiro, "A Theory of the Origins of the State," *Science* 169 (1970): 733–38; see also Sue Mansfield, *The Gestalts of War* (New York: Dial, 1982), 41–54.

29. This thought came to me in 1991 as what seemed at the time a farfetched fantasy. The Tesuque post office began tarring its parking lot and painted its first parking place in 1993.

30. Ehrenberg, *Women in Prehistory*, 87–88.

31. Robert Wenke, *Patterns in Prehistory* (New York: Oxford University Press, 1990), 326; and C. L. Redman, *The Rise of Civilization* (San Francisco: W. F. Freeman, 1978), 180.
32. Ponting, "Historical Perspectives on Sustainable Development," 6–9, 31–33.
33. Ehrenberg, *Women in Prehistory*, 99.
34. Wenke, *Patterns in Prehistory*, 240, 248.
35. Adele Getty, conversation, Santa Fe, N. Mex., 10 July 1991.
36. Adele Getty, *Goddess: Mother of Living Nature* (London: Thames and Hudson, 1990), 14–15.
37. Shepard, *Nature and Madness*, 38.
38. S. A. Rosen, "Notes on the Origins of Pastoral Nomadism: A Case Study from the Negev and Sinai," *Current Anthropology* 29, no. 3 (1988): 498–506.
39. M. K. Martin and D. Voorheis, *Female of the Species* (New York: Columbia University Press, 1975), chap. 10; K. Kristiansen, "Ideology and Material Culture: An Archaeological Perspective," in M. Spriggs, ed., *Marxist Perspectives in Archaeology* (Cambridge: Cambridge University Press, 1984); T. Larsson, *The Bronze Age Metalwork in Southern Sweden* (Umea, Sweden: Umea University Press, 1986); E. Friedl, "Society and Sex Roles," *Human Nature* 1 (1978): 68–75; and P. Draper, "!Kung Women: Contrasts in Sexual Equalitarianism in Foraging and Sedentary Contexts," in R. Reiter, ed., *Toward an Anthropology of Women* (New York: Monthly Review Press, 1975).
40. Ehrenberg, *Women in Prehistory*, 107.
41. Kristiansen, "Ideology and Material Culture."
42. American Psychiatric Association, *Diagnostic and Statistical Manual of Mental Disorders*, 3d ed. (Washington, D.C.: American Psychiatric Association, 1987), 238.

6. Discontents

1. Calvin Martin, *In the Spirit of the Earth* (Baltimore: Johns Hopkins University Press, 1992), 52.
2. Paul Shepard, *Nature and Madness* (San Francisco: Sierra Club Books, 1982), 31.
3. Simon Ortiz, *From Sand Creek* (Oak Park, N.Y.: Thunder's Mouth Press, 1981), 35.

4. Gerald Haslam, "Hawk's Flight: An American Fable," in Simon Ortiz, ed., *Earth Power Coming* (Tsaile, Ariz.: Navajo Community College, 1983), 147.

5. Sigmund Freud, *Civilization and Its Discontents* (New York: W. W. Norton, 1962), 91.

6. Lewis Mumford, *The Pentagon of Power* (New York: Harcourt Brace Jovanovich, 1970), 369.

7. R. D. Laing, *The Politics of Experience* (London: Penguin, 1967), 61–62.

8. Erich Fromm, *The Sane Society* (New York: Henry Holt, 1955), 15.

9. Abram Kardiner, *The Traumatic Neurosis of War* (New York: Hoeber, 1941), 82.

10. Kai Erikson, *Everything in Its Path* (New York: Simon and Schuster, 1976), 235.

11. Ibid., 242.

12. Robert Jay Lifton, *Death in Life: Survivors of Hiroshima* (New York: Basic Books, 1982), 31.

13. Robert Jay Lifton, *The Nazi Doctors* (New York: Basic Books, 1986), chap. 19; and Jerome Frank, *Sanity and Survival* (New York: Random House, 1967), 130–31, 182–85.

14. Stanley Diamond, *In Search of the Primitive* (New Brunswick, N.J.: Transaction Books, 1974), 158.

15. Erikson, *Everything in Its Path*, 164.

16. Erich Fromm, *The Anatomy of the Human Heart* (New York: Holt Rhinehart and Winston, 1973), 227–28.

17. Philip Slater, *The Pursuit of Loneliness* (Boston: Beacon Press, 1970), 5.

18. Frances Harwood, conversation, Tesuque, N. Mex., 1 August 1992.

1. Techno-Addiction

1. Craig Nakken, *The Addictive Personality* (San Francisco: Harper/Hazeldon, 1988), 4, 19–62.

2. Anne Wilson Schaef, *Co-Dependence* (San Francisco: Harper and Row, 1986), 21.

3. Jane Hollister Wheelwright, *The Ranch Papers: A California Memoir* (Venice, Calif.: Lapis Press, 1988); cited in Lorraine Anderson, *Sisters of the Earth* (New York: Vintage, 1991), 313.

4. Terry Kellogg, "The Roots of Addiction" (Lecture presented at the

Institute for Integral Development, Colorado Springs, Colo., August 1991).

5. Abram Kardiner, *The Traumatic Neurosis of War* (New York: Hoeber, 1941), 82–84.

6. Morris Berman, *The Re-enchantment of the World* (New York: Bantam, 1981), 242.

7. Al Gore, *Earth in the Balance* (Boston: Houghton Mifflin, 1992), 220.

8. Gregory Bateson, *Steps to an Ecology of Mind* (New York: Ballantine, 1972), 337.

9. Lewis Mumford, *Technics and Human Development* (New York: Harcourt Brace Jovanovich, 1966); and Lewis Mumford, *The Pentagon of Power* (New York: Harcourt Brace Jovanovich, 1970).

10. Lewis Mumford, "The Case against Modern Architecture," *Architectural Record* 131, no. 1 (April 1962): 157.

11. Jacques Ellul, *The Technological Society* (New York: Vintage, 1964), xxv, 5.

12. Lewis Mumford, *My Works and Days: A Personal Chronicle* (New York: Harcourt Brace Jovanovich, 1979), 9.

13. Chellis Glendinning, *When Technology Wounds: The Human Consequences of Progress* (New York: Morrow, 1990).

14. U.S. Environmental Protection Agency, *Unfinished Business: A Comparative Assessment of Environmental Problems* (Washington: EPA/Office of Policy Analysis, February 1987), 84–86; and Lawrie Mott and Karen Snyder, "Pesticide Alert," *Amicus Journal* 10, no. 2 (Spring 1988): 22.

15. David Maraniss and Michael Weiskoff, "Corridor of Death along the Mississippi," *San Francisco Examiner*, 31 January 1988; Jay Gould, *Quality of Life in American Neighborhoods* (Boulder, Colo.: Westview Press, 1986), 2.117–2.120.

16. "Underground Toxics Leak in Great Lakes and Threaten Residents," *Ground Water Monitor*, 24 December 1985.

17. Critical Mass Energy Project, *1986 Nuclear Power Safety Report* (Washington: Public Citizen, 1986); and D. F. Ford, *Three Mile Island* (New York: Penguin, 1982).

18. "Pesticide Maker Will Halt Chlordane Sales," *San Francisco Chronicle*, 12 August 1987; and "EPA's Handling of Chlordane Demonstrates FIFRA's Flaws," *Public Citizen*, November/December 1987.

19. "Pesticide Pollution," *Washington Spectator* 14, no. 5 (1 March 1988), 1–4.

20. U.S. Congress, House Subcommittee on Water and Power, testimony of Robert Becker, M.D., 22 September 1987.

21. U.S. Environmental Protection Agency, *Aerometric Information and Retrieval System: 1988/Supplemental Data from Regional Office Review* (Washington: EPA, July 1989).

22. Ralph Nader et al., *Who's Poisoning America? Polluters and Their Victims in the Chemical Age* (San Francisco: Sierra Club Books, 1981), 12; and *Science for the People*, January/February 1989.

23. Thich Nhat Hanh, *The Heart of Understanding* (Berkeley, Calif.: Parallax Press, 1988), 3.

24. Gregory Bateson, conversation with Frances Harwood, Boulder, Colo., August 1975. (Harwood told me of this conversation in Kerrville, Texas, on 24 May 1992.)

25. Ashley Montagu, *Touching* (New York: Columbia University Press, 1971), 67.

26. L. E. Holt, *The Care and Feeding of Children* (New York: Appleton-Century, 1935).

27. Susan Griffin, conversation, Berkeley, Calif., 25 March 1988.

28. Langdon Winner, *Autonomous Technology* (Cambridge: MIT Press, 1977), 135.

29. Michiel Schwarz and Rein Jansma, *The Technological Culture* (Amsterdam: De Bailie, 1989), 3.

30. Vine Deloria, *We Talk, You Listen* (New York: Delta, 1970), 185.

31. Winner, *Autonomous Technology*, 295–96.

32. Ivor Browne, "Psychological Trauma, or Unexperienced Experience," *ReVision* 12, no. 4 (Spring 1990): 21.

33. Kardiner, *The Traumatic Neurosis of War*, 81.

34. Browne, "Psychological Trauma," 27.

35. Paul Shepard, *Nature and Madness* (San Francisco: Sierra Club Books, 1982), 35.

36. James Hillman, "Peaks and Vales," in James Hillman, ed., *Puer Papers* (Dallas, Tex.: Spring Publications, 1979), 62.

8. We Create Our Own Reality

1. Jerry Mander, *In the Absence of the Sacred* (San Francisco: Sierra Club Books, 1991), 3–4.

2. Cited in Mark Dowie, "Brave New Tiny World," *California*, November 1988, 90.

3. Mander, *In the Absence of the Sacred*, 150–57.

4. Thomas Handloser, "An Interview with Godfrey Reggio," *THE Magazine* 1, no. 3 (September 1992): 10.

5. Mander, *In the Absence of the Sacred*, 150.

6. For alternative approaches to deconstructive postmodern philosophy, see Charlene Spretnak, *States of Grace* (San Francisco: Harper San Francisco, 1991); David Ray Griffin, ed., *Sacred Interconnections: Postmodern Spirituality, Political Economy and Art* (Albany, N.Y.: SUNY Press, 1990); and David Ray Griffin, ed., *Spirituality and Society: Postmodern Visions* (Albany, N.Y.: State University of New York Press, 1988).

7. Yvonne Dion-Buffalo and John Mohawk, "Thoughts from an Autochthonous Center," *Akwe:kon Journal* 9, no. 4 (Winter 1992): 19.

8. Walter Truett Anderson, *Reality Isn't What It Used to Be* (New York: Harper and Row, 1990), 3.

9. Ibid., 6.

10. Ibid., 13.

11. Theodore Roszak, *The Voice of the Earth* (New York: Simon and Schuster, 1992), 70.

9. The First Step

1. Judith Herman, *Trauma and Recovery* (New York: Basic Books, 1992), 155.

2. Alcoholics Anonymous, *The Big Book*, 3d ed. (New York: Alcoholics Anonymous World Services, 1976).

3. Thomas Handloser, "An Interview with Godfrey Reggio," *THE Magazine* 1, no. 3 (September 1992), 11.

4. Anne Wilson Schaef, *Escape from Intimacy* (San Francisco: Harper and Row, 1989), 152.

5. Nancy and the Chicago Punks, "Chicago," *Maximum Rock 'n Roll* no. 5 (March/April 1983).

6. Rasa Gustaitis, "Teenage Malaise," *California Living*, 16 January 1983.

10. Moose Becomes Me

1. Ivor Browne, "Psychological Trauma, or Unexperienced Experience," *ReVision* 12, no. 4 (Spring 1990): 32.

2. Jeannette Armstrong, "The Ones Who Are Dream and Land Together," *Elmwood Quarterly* 7, no. 3 (Fall Equinox 1991): 3.
3. Quoted in Elizabeth Roberts and Elias Amidon, eds., *Earth Prayers*
(San Francisco: Harper San Francisco, 1991), 95.
4. Stanley Diamond, *In Search of the Primitive* (New Brunswick, N.J.:
Transaction Books, 1987), 207.
5. T. M. Keare et al., "Implosive (Flooding) Therapy Reduces Symptoms of Post-Traumatic Stress Disorder in the Vietnam Combat
Veteran," *Behavior Therapy* 20 (1989): 245–60; and A. J. Cienfuegos
and C. Morelli, "The Testimony of Political Repression as a Therapeutic Instrument," *American Journal of Orthopsychiatry* 53 (1983):
43–51.
6. Vine Deloria, *We Talk, You Listen* (New York: Delta, 1970).
7. See Chellis Glendinning, "We Talk, You Listen," *New Age Journal*,
January/February 1993, 75–77, 120–24.

11. The Whole Story and Nothing but the Story

1. Judith Herman, *Trauma and Recovery* (New York: Basic Books, 1992),
184.
2. Deena Metzger, *Writing for Your Life* (San Francisco: Harper San
Francisco, 1992), 71.
3. George Steiner, *Language and Silence* (New York: Atheneum, 1967);
quoted in Bruno Bettelheim, *Surviving and Other Essays* (New York:
Vintage, 1980), 103.
4. Shana Penn, telephone conversation, 28 December 1992.
5. Bettelheim, *Surviving and Other Essays*, 246.
6. Deena Metzger, "Healing the Shoah," *Animus* 17, no. 1 (Fall 1990):
6–16; also, Deena Metzger, telephone conversation, 2 December
1992.
7. "Team IV Stories," *Veterans Vietnam Restoration Project* no. 14 (June
1992): 4.
8. "Team IV Stories," 6.
9. Jan Scruggs and Joel Swerdlow, *To Heal a Nation* (New York: Harper
and Row, 1985), 144, 153.
10. Ibid., 145.
11. Ibid., 147.

12. Earthgrief

1. See Joanna Rogers Macy, *Despair and Personal Power in the Nuclear Age* (Philadelphia: New Society Publishers, 1983); and Chellis Glendinning, *Waking Up in the Nuclear Age* (Philadelphia: New Society Publishers, 1987).
2. Deena Metzger, telephone conversation, 2 December 1992.
3. Jeannette Armstrong, "The Ones Who Are Dream and Land Together," *Elmwood Quarterly* 7, no. 3 (Fall Equinox 1991): 3.
4. Francisco Alarcón, "Cihuacoatl," in *Snake Poems* (San Francisco: Chronicle Books, 1992), 126.
5. Jai Lakshman, conversation, Ojo Caliente, N. Mex., 3 August 1989.
6. Quoted in speech by Colorado senator Tim Wirth, Clinton for President rally, Santa Fe, N. Mex., 1 November 1992.

13. Primal Matrix Re-Arising

1. Linda Hogan, "Mean Spirit (New York: Ivy Books, 1990), 262.
2. Rollo May, "Contributions to Existential Psychotherapy," in Rollo May et al., eds., *Existence: A New Dimension in Psychiatry and Psychology* (New York: Basic Books, 1958), 61.
3. Theodore Roszak, *The Voice of the Earth* (New York: Simon and Schuster, 1992), chap. 2.
4. Bil Gilbert, "Once a Malcontent, Ruby Has Taken Up Brush and Palette," *Smithsonian* 21, no. 9 (December 1990): 40–51.
5. Bill McKibben, *The Age of Missing Information* (New York: Plume, 1992).
6. Michael Soulé, "A Vision for the Meantime," *Wild Earth: The Wilderness Project*, special issue (1992): 8.
7. Carl Jung, *Memories, Dreams, Reflections* (New York: Vintage, 1963), 359.
8. Douglas Cardinal and Jeannette Armstrong, *The Native Creative Approach* (Penticton, Canada: Theytus Books, 1991), 37.
9. Phil Lucas and Philip Lane, *Healing the Hurts* (Santa Fe, N. Mex.: Phil Lucas Productions/Four Worlds Foundation, 1988); videotape.
10. Jordan Fisher-Smith, "Environmentalism of the Spirit," *Orion* 11, no. 3 (Summer 1992): 78–79.

11. Lynda M. Leonard, conversation, Santa Fe, N. Mex., 29 January 1993.

14. All My Relations

1. Harry Miller, *The Common Sense Book of Puppy and Dog Care*, 3d ed. (New York: Bantam, 1987), 1.
2. Joseph Spies, *The Compleat Cat* (New York: Crown, 1966), 26.
3. Bruce Butterfield (National Gardening Association), telephone conversation, 17 May 1993.
4. Lynda M. Leonard, conversation, Santa Fe, N. Mex., 29 January 1993.
5. Richard Katz, *Boiling Energy: Community Healing among the Kalahari Kung* (Cambridge: Harvard University Press, 1982), 189–90.
6. Sheldon Wolin and John Schaar, *The Berkeley Rebellion and Beyond* (New York: Vintage, 1970), 100.
7. Francisco Alarcón, "Bioneers," *Seeds of Change 1993 Catalog* (Santa Fe, N. Mex.: Seeds of Change, 1993), 63.
8. Joan Halifax, *Shaman* (New York: Crossroad, 1982), 26.
9. Scott Russell Sanders, "Telling the Holy," *Orion* 12, no. 1 (Winter 1993): 58.
10. Richard Erdoes, *Crying for a Dream* (Santa Fe, N. Mex.: Bear and Company, 1990), 3.
11. Marc Kasky, telephone conversation, 15 February 1993.
12. See Felicitas Goodman, *Where the Spirits Ride the Wind* (Bloomington, Ind.: Indiana University Press, 1990).
13. Johanna Maybury, lecture in Santa Fe, N. Mex. (January 15, 1993).
14. Halifax, *Shaman*, 5.
15. Black Elk, as told to John Niehardt, *Black Elk Speaks* (New York: Morrow, 1932).
16. Luisa Kolker, conversation, Santa Fe, N. Mex., 15 January 1993.

15. Our Wildest Dreams

1. "Future Seems Unpeaceful," *Albuquerque Journal*, 8 May 1992, 2.
2. Annette Kolodny, "Among the Indians: The Uses of Captivity," *New York Times Book Review*, 31 January 1993, 27.
3. Quoted in Alan Ereira, *The Elder Brothers* (New York: Alfred Knopf, 1990), 195–97.

4. Alcoholic Anonymous, *The Big Book*, 3d ed. (New York: Alcoholics Anonymous World Services, 1976).

5. Henry David Thoreau, *Walden and On Civil Disobedience* (New York: Harper and Row, 1965), 259.

6. Quoted in Langdon Winner, *Autonomous Technology* (Cambridge: MIT Press, 1977), x.

7. Gloria Orenstein, "Artists as Healers," in Irene Diamond and Gloria Orenstein, eds., *Reweaving the World: The Reemergence of Ecofeminism* (San Francisco: Sierra Club Books, 1990), 287.

8. Leon Shenandoah, conversation with Frances Harwood, Crestone, Colo., July 1991. (Harwood told me of this conversation in Tesuque, New Mexico, on 15 August 1992.)

9. Quoted in Steve Wall and Harvey Arden, *Wisdomkeepers* (Hillsboro, Oreg.: Beyond Words Publishing, 1990), 105.

Epigraph Sources

Page v.: Rainer Maria Rilke, *Duino Elegies*. I have been unable to locate the particular translation from which I long ago jotted down these lines from the ninth elegy, and I haven't found an English version that reveals the Earth in quite the same way.

Part One: Susan Griffin, *Woman and Nature* (New York: Harper, 1978), p. 220.

James Houston, ed., *Songs of the Dream People: Chants and Images from the Indians and Eskimos of North America* (New York: Athenaeum, 1972).

Chapter 1: Henry David Thoreau, "Walking," in *Thoreau's Vision: The Major Essays* (Englewood Cliffs, N.J.: Prentice-Hall, 1973).

Chapter 2: Joy Harjo, "Fire," in *What Moon Drove Me to This?* (Berkeley, Calif.: I. Reed Books, 1978).

Chapter 3: Simon Ortiz, *From Sand Creek* (New York: Thunder's Mouth Press, 1981), p. 35.

Douglas Cardinal and Jeannette Armstrong, *The Native Creative Process* (Penticon, B.C.: Theytus Books, 1991), p. 18.

Part 2: Elizabeth Roberts and Elias Amidon, eds., *Earth Prayers* (San Francisco: HarperSanFrancisco, 1991), p. 70.

Paul Shepard, *Nature and Madness* (San Francisco: Sierra Club Books, 1982), p. 120.

Chapter 4: David Byrne, "Once in a Lifetime." From the album *Stop Making Sense*, Sire Records, 1984.

Chapter 5: Andrew Schmookler, *Parable of the Tribes* (Boston: Houghton Mifflin, 1984), p. 186.

Chapter 6: William Matthews, "Civilization and Its Discontents," in *A Happy Childhood* (Boston: Little, Brown, 1982). First published in *Antaeus*.

Chapter 7: Terry Kellogg, on the sound recording "The Roots of Addiction" (Santa Fe, N.M.: Audio Awareness).

Chapter 8: John Trudell, "Somebody's Kid," from a song written by John Trudell and Jesse Ed Davis.

Part 3: Beth Brant, *Mohawk Trail* (Ithaca, N.Y.: Firebrand Books, 1985).

Chapter 9: David Rains Wallace, "Forever Forests," in *Greenpeace* 15:5, September/October, 1990, p. 10.

Chapter 10: Recorded by the author at the Nevada test site.

Chapter 11: Lindsay Holt, "The Penan," in *Crosswinds* 4:4 (March/April 1992), p. 17.

Chapter 12: Jane Hollister Wheelwright, *The Ranch Papers: A California Memoir* (Venice, Calif.: Lapis Press, 1988).

Part 4: Paula Gunn Allen, "Kopis'taya" in *Songs from This Earth on Turtle's Back: An Anthology of American Indian Writers*, edited by Joseph Bruchac (Greenfield Center, N.Y.: Greenfield Review Press, 1984).

Chapter 13: Martha Reben, *The Healing Wounds* (New York: Crowell, 1952).

Chapter 14: Judith Herman, *Trauma and Recovery* (New York: Basic Books, 1992), p. 133.

Francisco Alarcón, "In Xochitl in Cuitatl," in *Snake Poems* (San Francisco: Chronicle Books, 1992), p. 150.

Chapter 15: Calvin Martin, *In the Spirit of the Earth* (Baltimore: Johns Hopkins University Press, 1992), p. 130.

Harvey Arden and Steve Wall, *Wisdomkeepers* (Hillsboro, Ore.: Beyond Words Publishing, 1990), p. 105.

Credits

Index